Learn
Science!

Grades 3-4
Elementary Level

Author
David Evans

**Revised, Updated, and Adapted
to US Science Standards by**
Joan Wagner

DK PUBLISHING

An Invitation to *Learn Science!*

Learning science is a major component of the knowledge base needed to live and work in today's world. There is an old adage, "I hear and I forget; I see and I remember; I do and I understand." *Doing* is the basis of inquiry science, which uses a constructivist approach to learning, whereby knowledge is constructed from the experiences of the learner. The caveat here is that these experiences must both minimize and address misconceptions about the natural world. For example, we do not catch a cold from the cold, but from a virus. And heavier objects do not fall faster! All objects will fall at the same exact rate if there is no air resistance.

The three workbooks in this series stress an inquiry approach to learning the key ideas in science, while developing the skills needed to do this science. They support how science should be taught as described in the *National Science Education Standards* from the National Research Council (NRC) and the *Benchmarks for Science Literacy* from the American Association for the Advancement of Science (AAAS), and are meant to provide additional support to the learning of science whether at home or at school.

There are three learning levels for *Learn Science!*:
- Grades K–2 (Primary)
- Grades 3–4 (Elementary)
- Grades 5–6 (Intermediate)

Each lesson in these workbooks has the following sections:
- *Background knowledge:* A key idea in science is described and new science terms are explained.

- *Science activity:* These are all guided activities to explore science and develop the skills for doing science.

- *Science investigation:* These inquiry activities are learner directed. They provide the learner with the opportunity to elaborate or extend upon a key idea in science. **Investigations involving chemicals, electricity, sharp tools, human subjects, or an open flame must be monitored by an adult. Look for the safety icon ⓘ shown here for these types of investigations.**

- *Answer key:* This is located at the back of the book. This can be used to evaluate and monitor each lesson/activity.

The weblinks in the book are listed in a separate section:
- *Referenced websites:* Some of the science investigations use websites. All websites are organized in a chart by topic, book page, and URL.

Two support templates are found at the back of the book:
- *Inquiry template:* The young investigator should use this as a guide for carrying out the *Science investigation* described on each page.
- *Concept map graphic organizer:* This is used to develop the language of science and to evaluate the learning of new concepts. It should be used in every activity in which a new science term is introduced—these terms are italicized in the text.

Progress Chart

This chart lists all the topics in the book.
Once you have completed each page, stick a star
in the correct box below.

Page	Topic	Star	Page	Topic	Star	Page	Topic	Star
6	I know about living things	☆	13	I know about my skeleton	☆	20	I know that not all plants have flowers	☆
7	I know that plants are living things	☆	14	I know that other animals have bones	☆	21	I know about seeds	☆
8	I know that food helps keep me healthy	☆	15	I know what my muscles do	☆	22	I know how seeds get to new places	☆
9	I know about herbivores and carnivores	☆	16	I know how to keep my body healthy	☆	23	I know what seeds need to grow	☆
10	I know how to keep my teeth healthy	☆	17	I know how to keep plants healthy	☆	24	I know that there are different animal groups	☆
11	I know that different animals have different teeth	☆	18	I know what roots do	☆	25	I know that there are different plant groups	☆
12	I have felt my pulse	☆	19	I know that there are different types of leaves	☆	26	I can use an animal key	☆

 **When you see this symbol you need to take extra care -
ask an adult to supervise you.**

Page	Topic	Star	Page	Topic	Star	Page	Topic	Star
63	I know that some changes can be reversed	☆	75	I know where the pushing forces are	☆	87	I know how sound travels	☆
64	I know how to filter mixtures	☆	76	I know where light comes from	☆	88	I know how to keep sounds out	☆
65	I know how to separate mixtures	☆	77	I know which star is the brightest	☆	89	I know how whales hear each other	☆
66	I know how to make a bulb light up	☆	78	I know about transparent, translucent, and opaque materials	☆	90	I know that the Sun, Earth, and Moon are spheres	☆
67	I know how to use a switch	☆	79	I know how shadows are formed	☆	91	I know that Earth spins around	☆
68	I know which metals are attracted to a magnet	☆	80	I know how I see things	☆	92	I know that shadows from the Sun move during the day	☆
69	I know which is the strongest magnet	☆	81	I know why things shine	☆	93	I know that the Moon travels around Earth	☆
70	I know which poles repel each other	☆	82	I know how to catch sunlight	☆	94	I can explain night and day	☆
71	I know that pushes and pulls are forces	☆	83	I know that vibrations make sounds	☆	95	I can describe the phases of the Moon	☆
72	I know that blowing air is a force	☆	84	I know how to change the pitch of sound	☆			
73	I know which surface has the most friction	☆	85	I know what happens when air vibrates	☆			
74	I know the best shape for a boat	☆	86	I can make sounds louder	☆			

Once you have completed this book, you've earned the certificate at the back!

A question of life or death

Background knowledge

All living things carry out certain life activities. They *reproduce*, *grow*, and obtain food or *nutrition*. They all *respire* to obtain energy. Some respire by using gases from the air. All living things must *excrete* or get rid of the waste they produce. Living things also *move*. They may move to get food or run away from an enemy. Last, living things are *sensitive* to the environment around them. For example, some feel pain or heat.

Science activity

The words below describe some of the life activities of living things. Draw a line from each word to the picture that shows it happening.

Reproduces
Excretes
Respires
Grows
Feeds
Senses
Moves

Science investigation

Place some pill bugs or crickets in a large covered jar with holes in the lid. (Websites **6-1**, **6-2**, and **6-3** have information about these critters.) Add a cut up potato and some fish food. Observe the critters and note down all of their life activities. Do they engage in every activity? Design and conduct an experiment to determine the critters' sensitivity to their environment.

Living it up with plants

Background knowledge

Plants are living things, but they are different from animals. Plants can make their own food inside their leaves. In order to make food, they need sunlight, gas from the air, and water from the soil. Plants use this food to grow and to carry out other life activities. They reproduce to make more plants like themselves. Unlike animals, plants do not move from place to place on their own. Plants are sensitive to light and grow toward it.

Science activity

Here are some observations about an oak tree. Put a check mark (✔) beside any fact that tells you the oak tree is alive.

- [ ] The tree uses its leaves to make food.
- [ ] Birds nest in the branches.
- [ ] It takes in water through its roots.
- [ ] The branches move in the wind.
- [ ] It produces acorns in the autumn.
- [ ] Squirrels eat the acorns.
- [ ] It grows 300 mm each year.

Acorns

Oak tree

Science investigation

Design and conduct an experiment to learn about a plant's life activities. How does it respond to its environment? How do you know it grows? Create your own questions to test. You might grow acorns with help from website **7-1**, or plant red beans as instructed on website **7-2**.

Staying healthy

Background knowledge

All living things need food and water to stay alive. Foods such as milk, meat, fish, eggs, and nuts contain *proteins* that help you grow. Other foods, such as fruit, bread, and pasta, contain *carbohydrates* that give you energy to move and play. Fats such as oil, butter, and margarine also give you energy. Fruits and vegetables contain important *vitamins* and *minerals* that keep you healthy.

Science activity

Here are some of the foods that Jeremy found in the kitchen. He read the labels to find out which foods contain fats and which contain proteins.

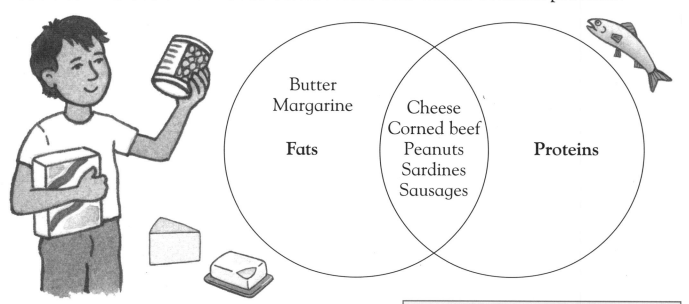

Butter
Margarine

Fats

Cheese
Corned beef
Peanuts
Sardines
Sausages

Proteins

Do any of the foods contain mainly fats? If so, which ones?

....

....

Do any of the foods contain mainly proteins? If so, which ones?

....

....

Which foods will help Jeremy to grow?

....

....

Science investigation

Play the food pyramid game on website **8-1**. First do the tour, then play the game. Now keep a log of what you eat for one week. Draw pictures of the food and the size of your portions. How healthy is your diet? Could you make it healthier? Website **8-2** has more information on good nutrition.

Munchtime for animals

Background knowledge

Many animals get the proteins, fats, and carbohydrates they need by eating plants. These animals are called *herbivores*. Some animals catch and eat other animals. These meat eaters are called *carnivores*. Carnivores have special features to help them catch and kill their prey. For example, hawks and owls have excellent vision that lets them see their prey from a distance. Go to websites **9-1**, **9-2**, and **9-3** to read more about different types of animals.

Science activity

The animals below are all carnivores. Draw a ring around the parts of each animal that help it catch and kill its prey.

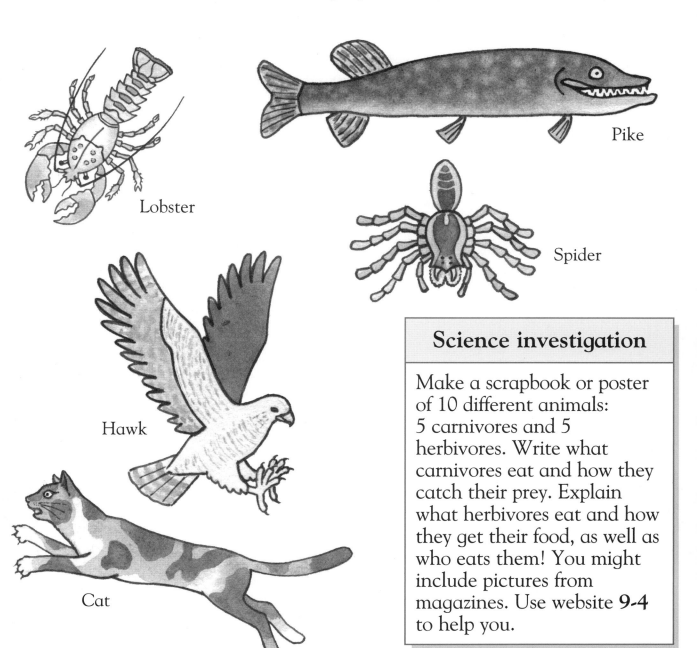

Lobster

Pike

Spider

Hawk

Cat

Science investigation

Make a scrapbook or poster of 10 different animals: 5 carnivores and 5 herbivores. Write what carnivores eat and how they catch their prey. Explain what herbivores eat and how they get their food, as well as who eats them! You might include pictures from magazines. Use website **9-4** to help you.

Rotten teeth

Background knowledge

When we chew food, some of it gets stuck between our teeth. Tiny living things in our mouths, called *bacteria*, attack this food and feed on it themselves. In fact, there are more bacteria in your mouth than there are people on our planet! The bacteria form large colonies on your teeth called *plaque*. As the bacteria feed, they produce acids, which cause decay. By cleaning your teeth after meals, the bits of food are brushed away so the bacteria cannot feed and produce acid. Go to websites **10-1** and **10-2** to learn more.

Science activity

A group of school children were expecting to see the school dentist. Their teacher asked them to do a survey of how often they cleaned their teeth. The block graph below shows the results of their survey.

How often we clean our teeth

Never						
Not very often	Sean	Sam				
Sometimes	James	Amy				
Most days	Oliver	Aziz	Emily	Maria		
Twice each day	Mina	John	Ling	Emma	Earl	Rachel

Which children are most likely to need treatment from the dentist?

....

Bite on this!

Background knowledge

You have different teeth for doing different jobs. The sharp front teeth, called *incisors*, bite and cut up food. The flat teeth, called *molars*, grind food before it is swallowed. You also have pointed teeth near the front of your mouth that grip and pierce food. These are called *canines*. Animals such as tigers and lions have large canines to catch and kill prey. Go to websites **11-1** and **11-2** to learn more about animal teeth.

Science activity

An animal's skull clearly shows its teeth. Look at the teeth on the rabbit skull and the cat skull below.

Rabbit skull

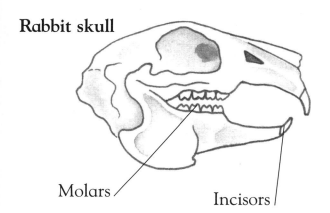

Molars

Incisors

Cat skull

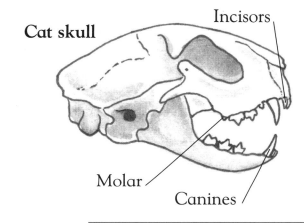

Incisors

Molar

Canines

Why does the rabbit have large incisors?

....

Why doesn't the rabbit have canines?

....

How can you tell that the cat catches and eats other animals?

....

Why does the cat have such small incisors?

....

....

Science investigation

Go to website **11-3** to compare human teeth with those of other animals. Compare the teeth of herbivores, carnivores, and omnivores on website **11-4**. Now look at your teeth in a mirror. How many of each type of teeth do you have? Are you an omnivore, herbivore, or carnivore?

The pulse of life

Background knowledge

When your heart beats, it pumps blood to parts of your body through vessels called *arteries* and *veins*. Arteries carry blood away from your heart to the rest of your body, while veins return blood to your heart. Where an artery crosses a bone, you can press a finger against your skin to feel the blood pumping. This is called your pulse. It is a measure of how fast your heart is beating. A child's pulse is usually about 70 to 80 beats per minute.

Science activity

A doctor found that a girl's pulse was 80 beats per minute. After running slowly for 1 minute, her pulse went up to 120 beats per minute. After skipping for another minute, her pulse was 170 beats. After resting for 2 minutes, her pulse was 140 beats.

Using the chart below, draw a bar graph of the results. What effect does exercise have on the girl's pulse?

....

Pulse (number of beats per minute)	Resting	Running slowly	Skipping	Resting
170				
160				
150				
140				
130				
120				
110				
100				
90				
80				
70				
60				
50				
40				
30				
20				
10				
0				

Science investigation

Find your pulse by pressing your first two fingers against the underside of your wrist, below the thumb. Now go to website **12-1** to learn how to take and measure your pulse before and after exercise. Design and conduct an experiment to see how your pulse rate changes after exercise. Also try the activity on website **12-2**.

Bones provide great support!

Background knowledge

Inside your body is a *skeleton* made of *bones*. Bones mostly contain a material called *calcium*. Your skeleton protects the soft inner parts of your body. *Muscles* pull on parts of the skeleton to make your body move. A *joint* is a place where two bones meet. Some joints allow parts of the skeleton to bend. Your skeleton provides the support you need to give your body a shape— otherwise you would be a ball of jelly! Go to website **13-1** to learn more.

Science activity

Here is a picture of a human skeleton. On the picture draw the four arrows listed below, and label them A, B, C, and D.

Arrow A should point to the part of the skeleton that protects the brain.
Arrow B should point to the joint that allows the leg to bend at the knee.
Arrow C should point to the part that protects the lungs.
Arrow D should point to the part that protects the heart.

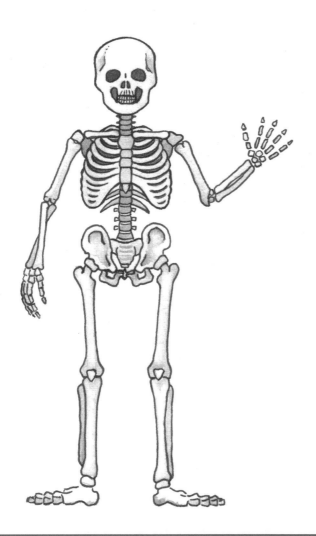

Science investigation

Trace your hand onto a piece of paper. Feel your bones and see if you can draw a map of the bones on your hand. Go to website **13-2** to put together an interactive skeleton and see if your drawing was correct. Website **13-3** contains craft activities about the human skeleton.

How 'bout them bones!

Background knowledge

Not all animals have bones. Animals with bony skeletons inside of them are called *vertebrates*. All vertebrates have a backbone. Vertebrates include humans, dogs, snakes, fish, and birds. Skeletons give protection and support to the body, and help it to move. Animals such as worms, insects, snails, and jellyfish do not have bony skeletons; they are called *invertebrates*.

Science activity

Here are the skeletons of a fish, a bird, and a frog. On each of the drawings, color in the part that protects the brain, and color in the backbone.

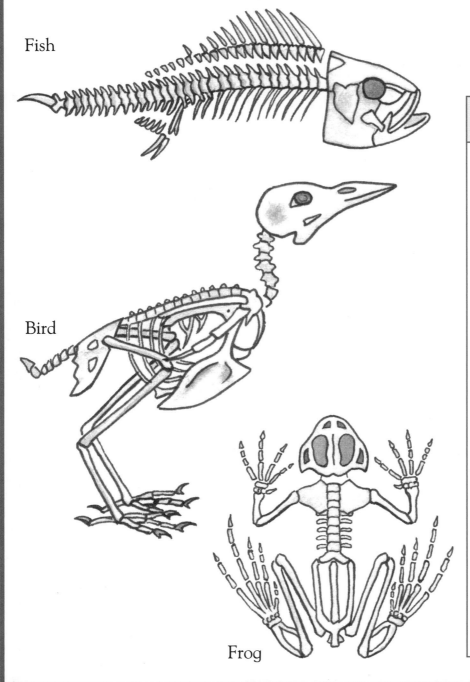

Fish

Bird

Frog

Science investigation

⚠ Ask an adult to remove the meat from a cooked beef bone and the wing, leg, and neck of a chicken. Trace the bones onto a piece of paper and label them. Draw an arrow to a joint on the chicken wing. How does a beef bone compare to a chicken bone? Is one harder than the other? Website **14-1** compares many different skeletons.

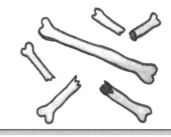

Can you make a muscle?

Background knowledge

The muscles all over your body move your skeleton. When muscles work, they get thicker and shorter. We say that muscles *contract*. When a person "makes a muscle," you seee their muscle contract. A contracting muscle pulls on a bone, making it move. Muscles need energy to work. They get their energy from sugars in your blood. Most muscles rest or relax after they have been used. They get longer and flatter. The heart is a muscle that works very hard—every time you feel a pulse, your heart muscle has contracted! Go to website **15-1** to learn more.

Science activity

When you move your legs, feet, hands, or arms, the muscles that move them get thicker and shorter.

On picture A, draw arrows pointing to where you think the muscles moving the foot will get thicker.

On picture B, draw an arrow pointing to where you think the muscle raising the forearm will get thicker.

Movement of arm

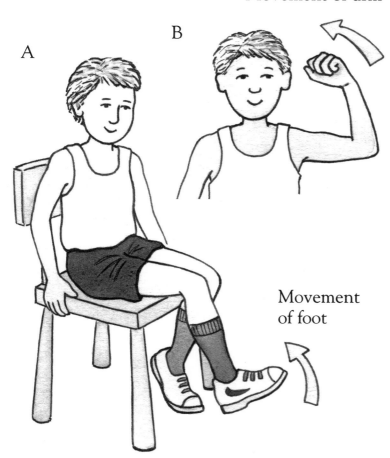

B

A

Movement of foot

Science investigation

Design and conduct an experiment to see how your muscles move your arms and legs. Which muscles thicken and shorten when you move different parts of your body? Go to website **15-2** to learn more about muscles and bones.

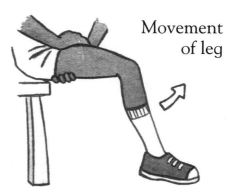

Movement of leg

The good and bad of drugs

Background knowledge

When you are ill, you may need to take medicines to help you get better. A doctor or pharmacist tells you what medicine to take. Medicines contain *drugs*, which have an effect on your body. Some of these drugs may reduce fever, coughing, and sneezing. Others may treat an upset stomach. Alcohol and nicotine in cigarettes are also drugs, but they are not medicines. In fact, they can harm or even kill you. Some drugs, such as heroin, cannabis, and cocaine, are considered so harmful that it is against the law to own or sell them.

Science activity

Which of these drugs would you normally get from a pharmacy or drugstore? Place a check mark (✔) by each one.

Wine ☐

Cough medicine ☐

Indigestion medicine ☐

Beer ☐

Headache pills ☐

Eye drops ☐

Antiseptic cream ☐

Cigarettes ☐

Science investigation

⚠ Take the quiz on website **16-1**. Ask an adult to show you the warning on a packet of cigarettes. Is the warning always the same on every brand? Go to website **16-2**. What are the health dangers of smoking? Design your own advertisement to prevent people from smoking.

Great to be green

Background knowledge

Using energy from the Sun, plants take gas from the air and water from the soil to make their food. They make sugar, and store it as starch. Plants need sunlight to make an important green substance called *chlorophyll*. Besides giving plants their color, chlorophyll captures *solar energy* for the plant to make food. Just like you cannot bake a cake without an oven, plants cannot make food without energy from the Sun. Plants absorb water through their roots. The water taken up by the roots contains important minerals that the plant needs to stay healthy.

Science activity

Gus wanted to find the best way to grow watercress. He took three dishes, put cotton wool in each one, and sprinkled watercress seeds over the cotton wool. He placed dishes A and B on a window ledge and dish C in a shoebox. He watered dishes A and C every day, but not dish B. This is how the dishes looked after two weeks. Label each dish A, B, or C to show which is which.

Dish ....
The seeds have not grown.

Dish ....
The seedlings have long, weak stems and small, pale-yellow leaves.

Dish ....
The seedlings have strong stems and large, dark-green leaves.

Science investigation

Design and conduct an experiment to see what effect temperature has on the growth of seeds. Use watercress seeds or bean seeds. Your refrigerator can be used for a cold place. Do the plant growth activity on website **17-1**.

Know your roots!

Background knowledge

Plants use their *roots* to hold themselves in the soil. The other main job of a root is to take in water and minerals from the soil. The plant uses the water to make its food. Some roots go down a long way into soil to find water. Other roots spread out widely to use the water around them. The roots of some plants become very thick because the plants store food in the root. When you eat carrots, you are eating one of many tasty and healthy roots.

Science activity

Shawna likes helping her mother in the garden. One of her favorite jobs is pulling weeds. Here are some weeds that she found.

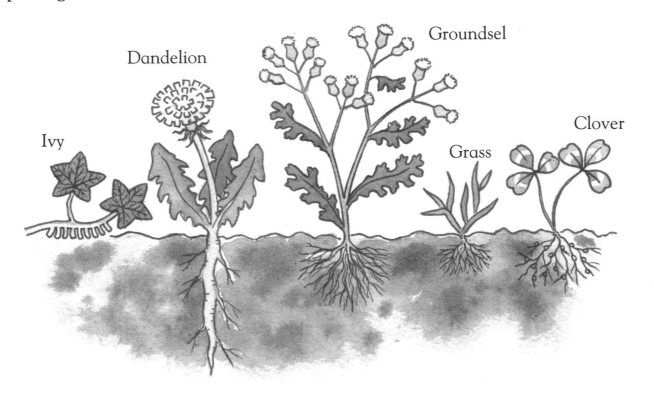

Groundsel

Dandelion

Clover

Ivy

Grass

Why is dandelion the hardest to pull up? ....

Why is ivy the easiest to pull up? ....

Science investigation

Do roots grow up or down? Soak four beans in water overnight. Place wet paper towels around a styrofoam cup. Pin the seeds in different positions on the cup and cover with a see-through plastic bag. Observe and record what happens. See website **18-1**. Do the activity on website **18-2**.

Name that leaf

Background knowledge

Leaves are usually green because they have a green chemical inside of them called chlorophyll, which catches sunlight. They also have tiny holes on their surface to let air and water vapor in and out. Leaves use sunlight, air, and water to make food.

Science activity

Use this branching diagram to find out which tree each leaf comes from.

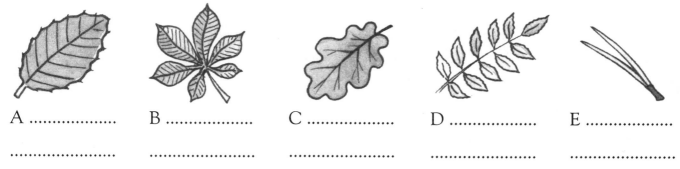

A ....

B ....

C ....

D ....

E ....

....

....

....

....

....

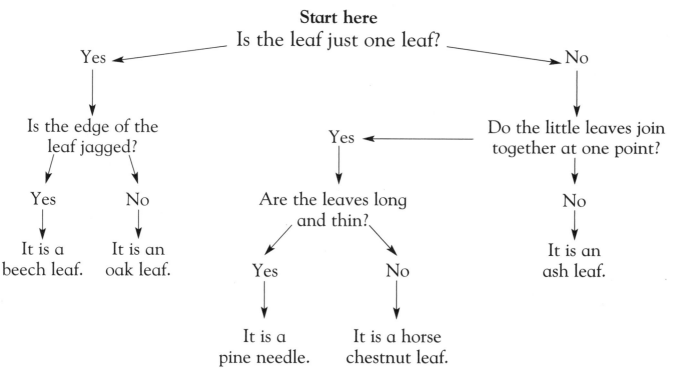

Start here
Is the leaf just one leaf?

Yes

No

Is the edge of the leaf jagged?

Do the little leaves join together at one point?

Yes

No

Yes

It is a beech leaf.

It is an oak leaf.

Are the leaves long and thin?

No

It is an ash leaf.

Yes

No

It is a pine needle.

It is a horse chestnut leaf.

Science investigation

(!) Collect some leaves. Try to choose mostly tree leaves if possible. Create your own way to sort them. Attach each group to a piece of paper and note down how the leaves are similar. Go to websites **19-1** and **19-2** to learn more.

Flower power

Background knowledge

Most plants produce *seeds* that grow into new plants. All seeds contain a baby plant, stored food, and a protective covering. The seeds of conifer trees grow into woody cones. The seeds of other plants grow inside flowers. Ferns and mosses have neither cones nor flowers. Instead, they have special parts that produce *spores*. The spore cases appear as small specks on the underside of the plant's leaves. Each spore can grow into a new plant.

Science activity

Some of the plants in the pictures below are flowering plants. Circle the flowers. Color the plant that procudes spores green, and the plant that produces cones brown.

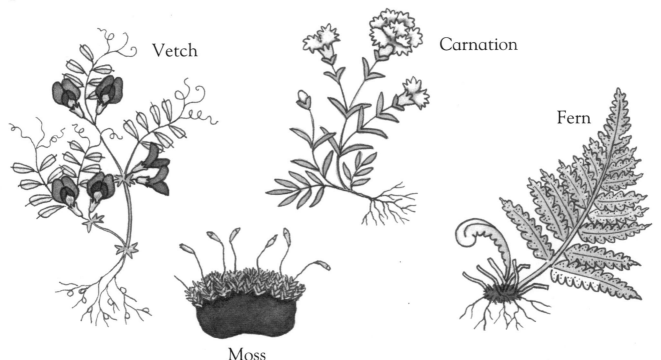

Vetch

Carnation

Fern

Moss

Cypress

Science investigation

Collect pictures of both flowering and non-flowering plants. Make a scrapbook of the plants. What are their names and where do they grow? Websites **20-1**, **20-2**, and **20-3** will help you. Complete the Venn diagram on **20-4**.

Seed detectives

Background knowledge

Seeds *germinate* (sprout) to grow into new plants. Many seeds are formed inside of flowers. Fruits then form around some seeds to protect them. There are many different kinds of fruits, some of which we eat. We eat nuts as well, which are seeds with a hard, woody shell. Some children are allergic to nuts. If they eat nuts they get very sick. Always ask an adult before you eat nuts.

Science activity

Be a seed detective! Which seed comes from which fruit? Draw a line from each fruit to its seed.

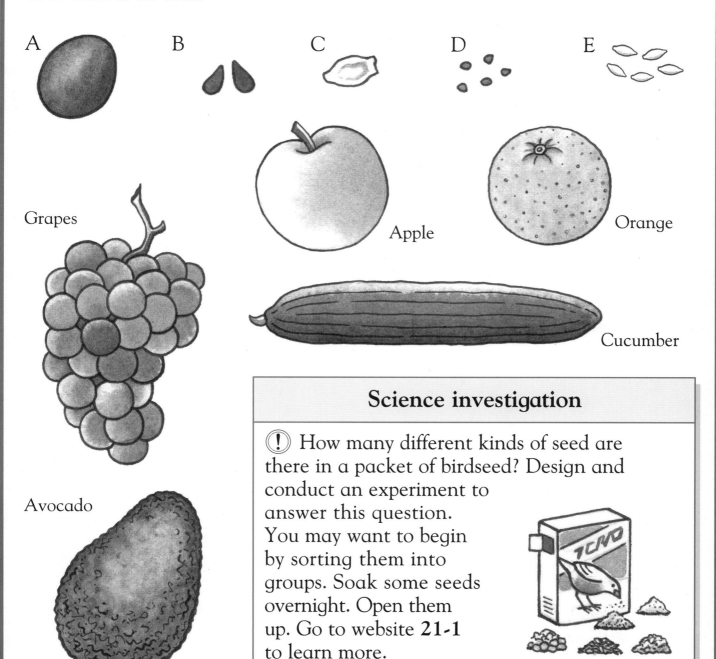

A

B

C

D

E

Grapes

Apple

Orange

Avocado

Cucumber

Science investigation

(!) How many different kinds of seed are there in a packet of birdseed? Design and conduct an experiment to answer this question. You may want to begin by sorting them into groups. Soak some seeds overnight. Open them up. Go to website **21-1** to learn more.

Seedy places

Background knowledge

Seeds need to be scattered so that new plants do not crowd around the parent plants. Some seeds are blown by the wind or carried by water. Others are sticky or prickly so that they stick to the fur or feathers of animals, who carry them to a new place. Some fruits burst open and spill out their seeds. Many seeds are inside brightly-colored or sweet fruits that attract animals to eat them. Then, the seeds are excreted by the animals in a different place, where they germinate into a new plant.

Science activity

Here are some seeds and fruits that are scattered by the wind. Use the yes/no key to find the names of the plants from which they come.

Clue 1 Does the seed have a parachute of fine hairs? If yes, go to clue 2.
         Does the seed have a flat wing? If yes, go to to clue 3.
Clue 2 Is the seed joined to the parachute by a stalk? If yes, it is a dandelion.
         If the seed is joined directly to the parachute, it is a willow herb.
Clue 3 Does the seed have two wings? If yes, it is a sycamore.
         Does the seed have one wing? If yes, go to clue 4.
Clue 4 Is the seed at the bottom of the wing? If yes, it is an ash.
         Are the seeds above the wing? If yes, it is a lime.

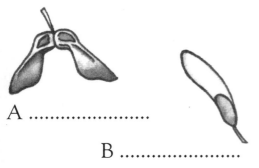

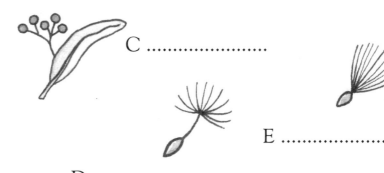

A ....

B ....

C ....

D ....

E ....

Science investigation

(!) Does the size of a fruit determine how many seeds are in the fruit? Design and conduct an experiment to answer this question. Use pumpkins if it is fall. Go to website **22-1** to do more pumpkin science.

Needy seeds

Background knowledge

Seeds need water to grow into new plants. Water causes seeds to swell, which cracks their protective coating. This allows the baby plant to get out of the seed. Some seeds need to be kept in a warm place before they will start to grow, while others germinate best if they are kept cool. Seeds do not need to be given food, since there is food stored in them.

Science activity

Here are a number of beans that have been planted in different ways.

Bean A is planted in sand but not watered.

Bean B is planted in soil and watered every day.

Bean C is planted in soil but not watered.

Bean D is planted on cotton wool and watered every day.

Bean E has no soil or water.

Which beans do you think will grow?

....

Why did you make this choice?

....

....

Science investigation

Design and conduct an experiment to see if light is needed for the growth of bean seeds. Make sure to use a good sample size of beans. Do the activity on website **23-1** to see what plants need to grow and stay healthy.

That's my type of animal!

Background knowledge
There are many different types of animals. Some look alike and some look quite different from one another. One way we can group animals is by the features they have in common. For example, animals that are warm blooded, lay eggs, lack teeth, and have feathers on their body and scales on their legs belong to a group of animals called birds. Go to website **24-1** to learn more.

Science activity
What features do the animals in each group have in common?
What is the name of each group of animals?

Common features of group A animals:

....

....

....

....

These animals are ....

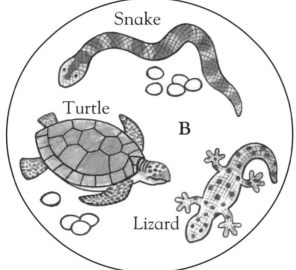

Common features of group B animals:

....

....

....

....

These animals are ....

Science investigation

Place some stuffed animals or animal toys together. Design and conduct an experiment to group them by their features. How many groups did you make? What features did you use? Compare your groups to the groups in the activity above. Visit the electronic zoo on website **24-2**.

Plant groups

Background knowledge

There are many different types of plants. Some look alike and some appear quite different from one another. Plants can be grouped according to the features they have in common. For example, plants that produce spores, contain chlorophyll, lack roots, and have feathery looking leaves are called ferns. Go to website **25-1** to learn more.

Science activity

What features do the plants in each group have in common? What is the name of each group of plants?

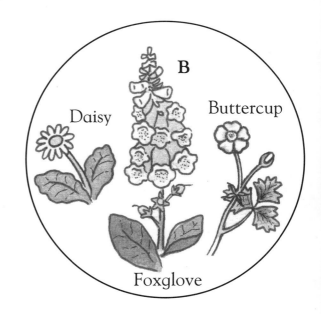

Cypress

Fir

A

Pine

Common features of group A plants:

....

....

....

....

These plants are ....

Common features of group B plants:

....

....

....

....

These plants are ....

B

Daisy

Buttercup

Foxglove

Science investigation

Compare the characteristics of two or more flowers. Use real flowers or pictures of flowers. You might compare the number of petals or color of the flower. Go to website **25-2** to see a flower slide show.

Animal detective

Background knowledge

An animal key helps you to identify different animals. If you don't know an animal's name, a key will give you clues to identify it. Just like a detective uses clues to solve a mystery, you will use clues to identify an unknown animal.

Science activity

Follow this yes/no animal key to find the names of the insects in the pictures.

Clue 1   Does the insect have very large eyes? If yes, go to clue 2.
           Does the insect have small eyes? If yes, go to clue 3.

Clue 2   Are the insect's eyes touching? If yes, it is a dragonfly.
           If the insect's eyes are not touching, it is a damselfly.

Clue 3   Does the head have a long pointed beak? If yes, it is a scorpion fly.
           If the head does not have a pointed beak, go to clue 4.

Clue 4   Does the insect have three tails? If yes, it is a mayfly.
           Does the insect have only one tail? If yes, it is a lacewing fly.

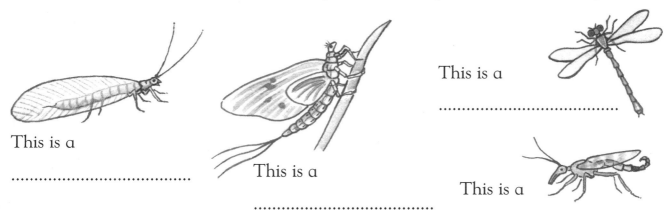

This is a

....

This is a

....

This is a

....

This is a

....

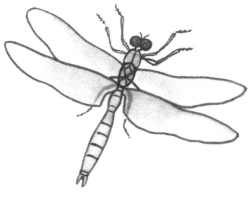

This is a

....

Science investigation

Click on "sorter 2" to complete the key on website **26-1**. Butterflies are often very attractive insects. Go to website **26-2** and click on your state to learn about the butterflies found where you live. Make a booklet listing 1–2 main features of each butterfly.

Plant detective

Background knowledge

By using a plant key, you can become a plant detective and discover the names of different plants. The plant key gives you clues to help identify a plant. The key shown below is a branching key. Each branch asks a question that requires a yes or no answer. As you move through the key, you will discover the name of the plant.

Science activity

Use this branching key to find the names of these fruits.

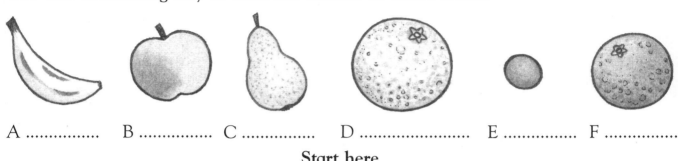

A ....   B ....   C ....   D ....   E ....   F ....

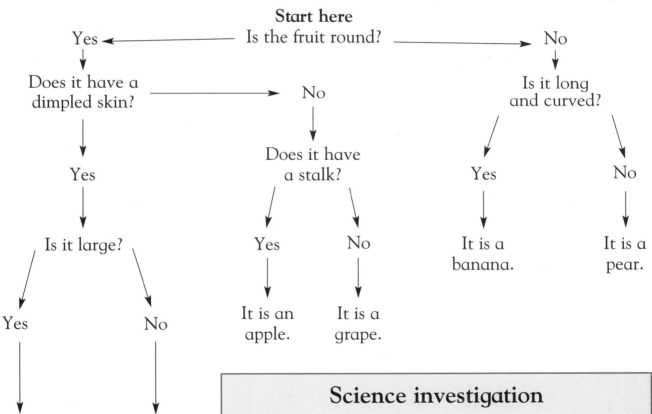

Science investigation

Obtain samples of different types of squash. Go to website **27-1** to help you make your own branching key to identify them. Use the pictures on the website if you cannot find squash. Website **27-2** has more key-reading practice.

Be kind to Mother Nature!

Background knowledge

The activities of humans can affect the lives of plants and animals. *Pollution* from factories and cars can poison the air and water that plants and animals need to survive. See website **28-1** for more information on pollution. When housing developments, roads, and malls are built, there is less open space for wildlife. Plants and animals need room to grow and reproduce. Humans also need to live and work, but there must be a balance between human needs and the needs of plants and animals. Mother Nature is not happy when the balance is disturbed!

Science activity

Draw a circle around each thing in this picture that could cause harm to animals and plants.

Science investigation

(!) Learn about local air pollution by attaching some masking tape, sticky side facing the air, to the outside of a window on each side of your house. Leave it there a week. Then use a magnifying glass to look at the tape. Compare it to fresh tape. What can you observe? Explain. Website **28-2** explains how human activity affects the air.

Animal homes

Background knowledge

Animals can be found living in almost any place on Earth. The place where an animal normally lives is called its *habitat*. There are many different kinds of habitats, such as in grass, under the ground, in trees, in ponds or rivers, on the seashore, and in the ocean.

Science activity

Where would these animals normally live? Draw a line between each animal and its habitat.

Pond

Worm

Water snail

Stickleback

Centipede

Crab

Frog

Rabbit

Mackerel

Millipede

Butterfly

Starfish

Woodpecker

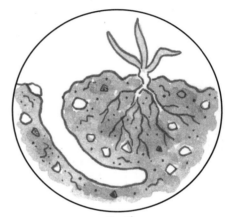

Soil

Ocean

Woodland

Science investigation

Go to websites **29-1** and **29-2** to learn about types of habitats. Do the activities on the websites **29-3** and **29-4**. Create a poster about one type of habitat. Include the plants and animals that live in the habitat. What type of habitat is it? What is the source of food and shelter for the animals?

Animals must fit in

Background knowledge

Animals live in many different habitats. Each animal's body is adapted to live in a certain habitat. For example, birds that live in water have webbed feet. Mammals breathe the air with lungs, while fish have gills for breathing under water. A mole has spade-like feet to help it dig through soil. All these special features are *adaptations* animals have that help them survive in their environment.

Science activity

Tadpoles are pond animals that hatch from eggs laid by frogs in the spring. Three parts of a tadpole's body are named below. In the spaces provided, write down how you think each part helps the tadpole to live in a pond.

Part of the body	How it helps the tadpole to live in a pond
Gills	....
Tail	....
Eyes	....

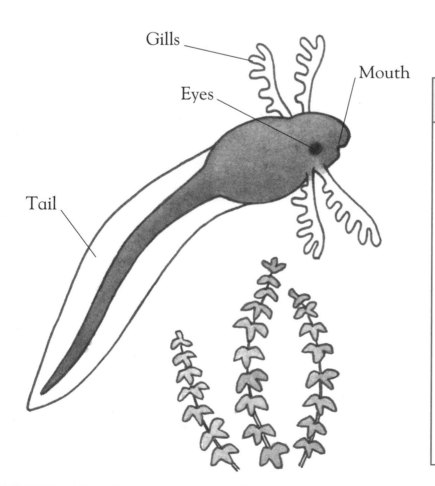

Gills

Eyes

Mouth

Tail

Science investigation

(!) Brine shrimp are related to shrimp and can easily be hatched. Their eggs can be purchased at a pet store. Hatch some brine shrimp (see website **30-1**), and with the help of a magnifying glass describe how they are adapted to their environment. Go to website **30-2** to learn more about animal adaptations.

Dinnertime for animals

Background knowledge

When animals feel hungry, they need to eat. Food provides the animals with carbohydrates, faats, and proteins, which are important nutrients they need to grow and live. Some animals have to hunt for their food while other animals eat mostly plants. Plants can make their own food using sunlight and gases from the air and water. Animals that eat plants are called *herbivores*. Animals that eat herbivores are called *carnivores*.

Science activity

Can you spot the herbivores in this group of animals? Write their names in the box.

Slug

Spider

Woodlouse

Caterpillar

Thrush

Ladybug

Deer

Rabbit

Herbivores

....

....

....

....

....

Science investigation

Go to website **31-1** to compare the skull and teeth of carnivores and herbivores. How do they differ? Draw a picture that compares their teeth. Make paper puppets of carnivore and herbivore dinosaurs from website **31-2**. Write and act out a play that shows how dinosaurs eat.

Food chains and webs

Background knowledge

All living things depend on one another for food. Plants make their own food. Some animals eat plants, and other animals eat animals that eat plants. Plant-eaters are called herbivores and animal-eaters are called carnivores. Some animals eat both plants and animals. They are called *omnivores*. The way in which living things depend on one another for food can be summarized in a *food chain* or a *food web*. An arrow is drawn to the living thing that is eaten by another living thing. Do the activity on website **32-1** to learn more.

Science activity

Look at the pictures, and find the animals or plants that complete these food chains. Write their names in the spaces on the chart.

Plant makes food	Herbivore eats plant	Carnivore eats herbivore
Pansy	....	Thrush
Seaweed	Periwinkle	....
....	Caterpillar	Robin
Grass	....	....

Seagull

Slug

Oak leaf

Human

Cow

Science investigation

Draw a food chain that shows a plant, an herbivore, and a carnivore. Use arrows to point to the animal doing the eating. You can use the information on website **32-2** to help you draw food chains in certain habitats.

Food to die for

Background knowledge

When living things die, other living things feed on them. If they have a skeleton or shell, it will be the only part left after all the soft parts are eaten. Earthworms feed on dead plants. Other animals, such as the maggots of flies, feed on dead animals. There are also tiny living things called *microbes* that feed on dead plants and animals. Bacteria and some fungi are microbes. When dead things *decay*, they are really being eaten by microbes!

Science activity

Here are some animals found in woodlands, where there are decaying leaves. Can you use this yes/no key to find their names?

Clue 1   Does the animal have six legs? If yes, it is a springtail.
           Does the animal have more than six legs? If yes, go to clue 2.
Clue 2   Does it have eight legs? If yes, it is a harvestman.
           Does it have more than eight legs? If yes, go to clue 3.
Clue 3   Does it have a broad, flat body? If yes, it is a woodlouse.
           Does it have a long, thin body? If yes, go to clue 4.
Clue 4   Does each section of the body have two legs? If yes, it is a centipede.
           Does each section of the body have four legs? If yes, it is a millipede.

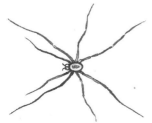

This is a ....

This is a ....

This is a ....

This is a ....

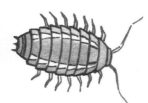
This is a ....

Science investigation

(!) Design and conduct an experiment to see what factors in the environment can affect the decay of an apple core. Examples of some factors are temperature, light, and moisture. Only one factor should be tested at a time. See website **33-1**.

Bad microbes

Background knowledge

Microbes such as viruses, bacteria, and fungi can infect living things and make them sick. They can cause illness and disease in humans. In some cases, the illness can kill people. Our bodies have special cells that fight microbes and help us get better. Medical doctors can give us medicines called *antibiotics* to help our bodies fight some harmful microbes. Antibiotics cannot treat viral infections. Go to website **34-1** to learn more about microbes.

Science activity

Write the letter **M** in the box beside each person infected with a microbe.

Cold ☐

Toothache ☐

Sprained ankle ☐

Chicken pox ☐

Broken arm ☐

Science investigation

⚠ Go to website **34-2** to learn about the importance of washing your hands. Make a poster for your room or classroom about this. Go to website **34-3** and take the hand washing quiz. Try some of the experiments on this website.

The good microbes

Background knowledge

Not all microbes are harmful; some are extremely useful. Microbes help the remains of plants and animals to decay. This returns important nutrients to the soil that plants will use to grow. Some microbes are used to make foods such as yogurt and cheese. A microbe called yeast is used to make bread. Yeast is also used to make alcohol. Bacteria convert sugars in some fruit juices to vinegar that is used in salad dressing.

Science activity

Put a check mark (✔) beside the drinks that are made with the help of useful microbes.

Wine ☐

Orange juice ☐

Beer ☐

Mineral water ☐

Yogurt drink ☐

Cola ☐

Science investigation

Make your own yogurt! Place a teaspoon of plain yogurt into a cup of milk. Cover the container and keep it in a warm place overnight. What is the evidence that yogurt formed? What causes yogurt to form? Always wash your hands after handling food. Go to website **35-1** for more information.

Material things

Background knowledge

Our world is made of many different types of material. Metals come from rocks. Wood comes from trees. Plastic and glass are made in factories. Ceramics are made from mud and clay. Natural fabrics are made from plants or animals, while synthetic fabrics are made in factories. We use all of these materials to build our homes and to make the things we use every day.

Science activity

Anna is blindfolded. Jim is describing four different types of material to her. Anna has to guess what type of material is being described. See how well you can do!

Material one does not feel cold. It is brown. It has a natural smell. When hit with a hammer, it makes a dull thud sound.

The matter is ....

Material two does not feel cold. It can be almost any color. It has a slight chemical smell. When hit with a hammer, it makes a dull clunk.

The matter is ....

Material three feels cold. It is shiny and silver in color. When hit with a hammer, it makes a ringing noise.

The matter is ....

Material four feels cold and is smooth. You can see through it. It has no smell. When hit by a hammer, it breaks.

The matter is ....

Science investigation

Write three "clue" descriptions for materials in your home. Hide the materials in a shoebox. Read one clue out loud at a time The person who needs the least number of clues to guess the material wins the game. Do the activity on website **36-1**.

A key to trees

Background knowledge
Wood is a natural material. It comes from the trunks and branches of trees.
Different trees produce different types of wood. Some woods, such as oak, are
very hard. Others, such as balsa, are very soft. Most woods can float, but
there are some that can sink, such as ebony. Wood has a distinctive smell.
When you hit it with a hammer, it has a distinctive sound.

Science activity
Use this yes/no key to work out which twig is from which tree in the picture
shown below. If you answer *no* to a question, move on to the next clue.

Clue 1: Does the twig have a single oval bud at the tip? If yes, it is from the
        horse chestnut.
Clue 2: Does the twig have black buds? If yes, it is from the ash.
Clue 3: Does the twig have lots of buds at the tip? If yes, it is from the oak.
Clue 4: Does the twig have long, thin buds? If yes, it is from the beech.
Clue 5: Does the twig have one striped bud at the tip? If yes, it is from the plane.

A ....   B ....   C ....   D ....   E ....

....

Science investigation

(!) Collect four samples of different woods that have
not been stained or varnished. Place about six drops
of blue food coloring into a cup of water. Brush each
piece of wood with the mixture. Compare and
contrast the way the woods look. Next, after the
wood is dry, make an impression of it in rolled-out
clay or playdough. Compare and contrast the
impressions each wood leaves behind.

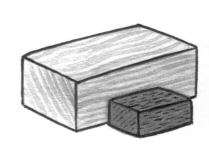

Metals shine

Background knowledge

There are many different *metals*, but they all have some things in common. All metals look shiny. They all allow electricity to pass through them. They can be pulled into wires. They can be flattened into thin sheets, such as aluminum foil. They feel cool when touched and get very hot when heated. A block of metal will make a ringing sound when hit. Some metals are attracted to magnets.

Science activity

Lindsay and Lisa did some experiments to find out the properties of different objects. They noted down their results in the table below.

Experiment	Object 1	Object 2	Object 3	Object 4	Object 5	Object 6
Is it attracted to a magnet?	Yes	No	No	No	No	No
Can electricity pass through it?	Yes	Yes	Yes	No	No	Yes
Does it feel cold?	Yes	Yes	No	No	No	Yes
Does it look shiny?	Yes	Yes	No	Yes	No	Yes

Write down the numbers of the objects that were made from metal.

....

Science investigation

(!) Ask an adult to help you build an electrical circuit with a battery, a bulb, and some wires. Cover the battery connection with different materials before connecting it to the wire. Observe if the bulb lights up. Remember, metal allows electricity to pass through it.

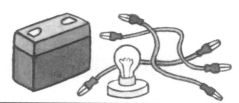

Are beds made of balsa wood?

Background knowledge

Some woods, such as ebony, are so hard that it is almost impossible to saw or knock a nail into them. Balsa wood is so soft you can easily break it with your fingers. Different woods are used to make different types of furniture, depending on how strong the furniture needs to be. Would you make your bed out of balsa wood?

Science activity

A class of children did a survey of furniture that had been attacked by woodworms. (Woodworms are beetle grubs that eat their way through timber, leaving tiny holes in the wood.) All of the furniture had been stored in the same room. Here are the results of the survey.

Furniture	Number of woodworm holes
Mahogany dressing table	15
Beech chair	20
Pine wardrobe	25
Teak sideboard	6
Oak table	10
Ebony stool	0

Which wood do woodworms find the hardest to bore through?

....

Which is the softest wood?

....

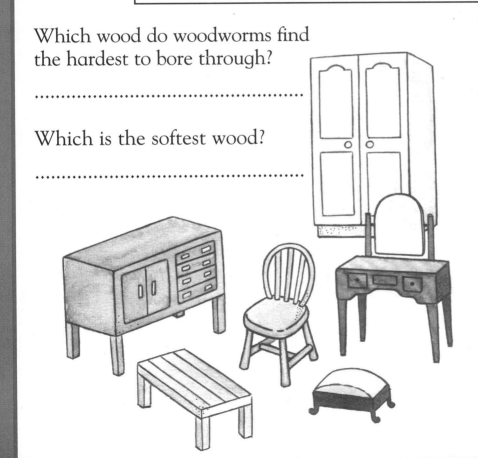

Science investigation

(!) Collect samples of different types of wood. Design and conduct your own experiment to decide which is the hardest wood. You might test how long it takes to hammer a nail into each wood. An adult should help you.

Can you bag it?

Background knowledge

Polyethylene is used to make plastic food bags in factories. Some food bags are see-through, so that you can see what is inside them. Others are thicker to protect food in the freezer. Millions of plastic grocery bags are made each day, and most are thrown away after use.

Science activity

Before ordering new grocery bags, a supermarket manager and her staff tested different types of bags to see which one was the strongest. They carefully added cans of beans to each bag until the handles began to tear. Here are their results.

Bag	Number of cans
Type A	23
Type B	20
Type C	40
Type D	12
Type E	20

Which bag do you think they ordered for their store? Explain.

....

....

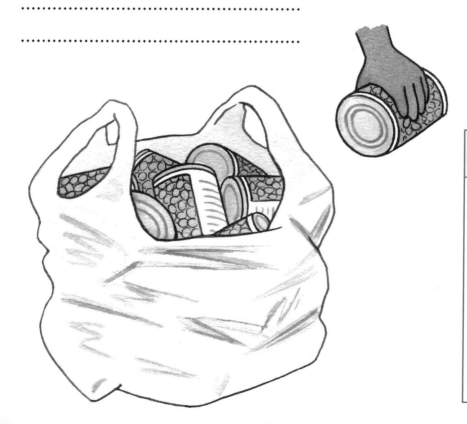

Science investigation

Is a paper bag stronger than a plastic bag? Design and conduct an experiment to answer this question. Use the Internet to see which type of bag is better for the environment.

It's flexible!

Background knowledge

Many materials bend when you push or pull on them. Materials that can be bent without breaking are called *flexible materials*. Very flexible materials will return to their original shape. Some materials are more flexible than others. *Rigid materials* do not bend at all, and may break easily if you try to bend them.

Science activity

Samantha and Maayan tested different materials to find out how flexible they were. First the height of each material was measured. Then a heavy object was placed on the material to squash it. After 1 minute, the object was removed. The height of the material was measured again. Here are the results.

Material	First measurement	Second measurement
Cube of Jell-O	3 cm	2.9 cm
Cube of modeling clay	10 cm	3 cm
Bath sponge	10 cm	10 cm
Cotton wool ball	3 cm	1.5 cm
Inflated balloon	20 cm	20 cm

Which is the most flexible material?

....

Which is the least flexible material?

....

Science investigation

(!) Collect samples of materials from around your home. Design and conduct an experiment to rate the flexibility of the samples you have collected. Have an adult help you, and wear safety glasses. Go to website **41-1** to learn more.

Attractive alloys

Background knowledge

An *alloy* is a solid mixture of metals, or of metals and nonmetals. Brass is an alloy of copper and zinc. It is used to make screws that do not rust. Bronze is an alloy of copper and tin. It is used to make bells and statues. Pennies are alloys made mostly of zinc and coated with copper. Nickels are made mostly of copper, and coated with nickel to make them silver. Stainless steel is an alloy of iron and chrome that is strong and slow to rust. Many baseball bats, golf clubs, and tennis rackets are made of alloys, which manufacturers use to make them strong but lightweight.

Science activity

Magnets will attract only the metals iron, nickel, and cobalt. The five objects below are all made from different alloys. Place a check mark in the box beside each one that you think will be attracted to a magnet.

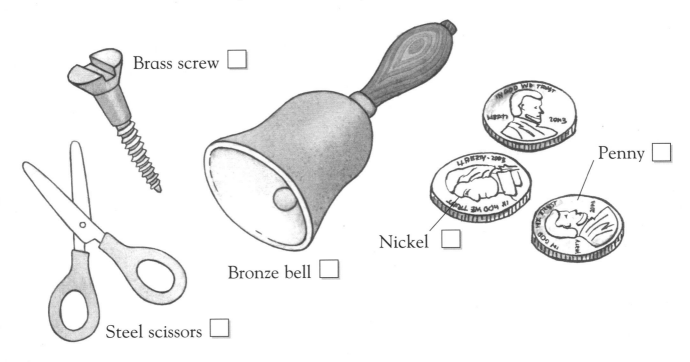

Brass screw ☐

Penny ☐

Nickel ☐

Bronze bell ☐

Steel scissors ☐

Science investigation

Collect samples of different solid objects. Can you tell by looking at them if they are alloys? Examine each object. Observe the properties of the object and record this information in a data table with three columns. In the first, record the name of the object. In the second, make a check mark if you think it is an alloy. In the third, explain your decision.

The good of wood

Background knowledge

We use a material to do a particular job because of its properties. For example, steel is used to make bridges because it is very strong. Aluminum is used to make foil wrap because it can be hammered into thin sheets. Wood has special properties that suit it to a wide range of jobs. These properties include flexibility, strength, and beauty.

Science activity

Some properties of woods are listed on the left, and some wooden objects are listed on the right. Draw a line to show which wood should be used to make each object.

Oak resists scratching. It does not make much noise when it is hit.

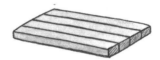

Wooden cheese board

Poplar has no smell. It is very light and looks clean.

Garden shed

Pine resists being squashed by a heavy load.

Living-room floor

Red cedar resists dampness.

Tunnel support in a mine

Science investigation

Paper is made from wood and can be used in many ways. Cardboard is used to make boxes. Paper towels wipe up messes. Collect different types of paper. Design and conduct an experiment to determine their properties. What do you think is the best use of each type? Go to website **43-1** to learn how to make recycled paper. Test your paper's properties.

All-weather gift wrap

Background knowledge

A material that soaks up water is said to be *absorbent*. A material that resists water or keeps water away is said to be *waterproof*. Rain boots are made of a plastic that is waterproof. Tissues are made of absorbent paper.

Science activity

Ling and Tyler wanted to find a material in which to wrap a present that was going to be mailed to a friend in another state. The present was a box of taffy, which would be ruined if it got wet. They needed to use a waterproof wrapping, so they decided to perform a test. First, they stretched five different materials over see-through containers. They then poured an equal amount of water onto each material.

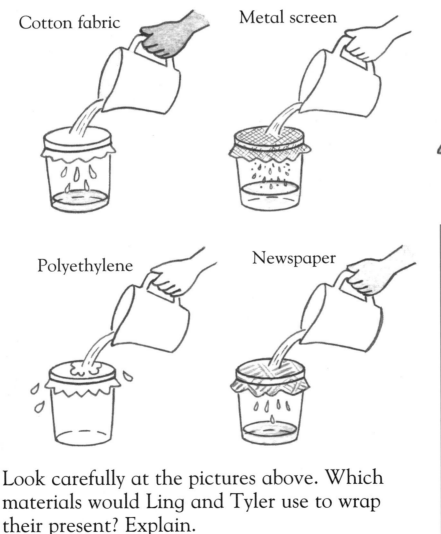

Cotton fabric

Metal screen

Aluminum kitchen foil

Polyethylene

Newspaper

Science investigation

Different types of wrap are used to keep food fresh. Design and conduct an experiment to determine which type is most waterproof.

Look carefully at the pictures above. Which materials would Ling and Tyler use to wrap their present? Explain.

....

....

Cool and not-so-cool materials

Background knowledge

Some materials, such as metal, feel cold when you touch them because they take heat away from your hand. When heat is taken away from you, you feel cooler. These materials are said to be good *thermal conductors*, as they are able to conduct heat. Other materials, such as wood, do not feel cold to the touch. They do not take heat away from your hand. These materials are *thermal insulators*. They are poor conductors of heat.

Science activity

Five spoons made of different materials were placed in a bowl. Five people each held a spoon while hot water was poured into the bowl. When a spoon became too hot to hold, the holder let go and said, "Now." Here are the results.

Type of spoon	How long it took to say "Now"
Plastic spoon	Did not say "Now"
Steel spoon	15 seconds
Wooden spoon	Did not say "Now"
Porcelain spoon	Did not say "Now"
Aluminium ladle	30 seconds

Which spoon is the best thermal conductor? Explain.

....

....

Science investigation

(!) Obtain five ice cubes of the same size. Use tongs to handle them so the heat of your hands does not melt them. Wrap each one in a different type of material and then place each ice cube in a small plastic bag. Rank the materials from best to poorest thermal insulator. Go to websites **45-1** and **45-2** to learn more.

How did you get those holes in your jeans?

Background knowledge

Fabrics are used around the house to make clothes, curtains, and towels. Fabrics such as cotton, linen, wool, and silk are made from natural fibers, which come from plants and animals. Fabrics can also be made of plastic, or a mixture of plastic and natural fibers. Fabrics have different properties. Some are tough, while other wear away quickly. Jeans are made of strong fabric, but even jeans get holes in them—usually near your knees!

Science activity

A scientist tested some fabrics to see how well they would stand up to rough wear. She took a piece of each fabric and rubbed it with some sandpaper. She counted how many times it had to be rubbed before the sandpaper made a hole in the fabric. Here is a table of her results.

Fabric	Number of rubs
Cotton	34
Cotton and terylene mixture	45
Pure wool	27
Wool and nylon mixture	30
Silk	12
Corduroy	53
PVC plastic	10

Which is the strongest fabric? Explain. ....

....

Science investigation

Obtain samples of different sewing threads. Design and conduct and experiment to see which thread is the strongest. Use data tables to record the results of each thread that you test.

Sponge it up

Background knowledge

Some materials, such as sponge, absorb water very well. These materials have spaces in which the water can be held. When a sponge is squeezed, the water in its small holes is forced out. There are many different kinds of sponges. Some sponges are natural, such as the sponge animals that live in the ocean. Most sponges purchased for home use are made in a factory. Some types of sponges can hold more water than others.

Science activity

Here are the results of some tests carried out on sponges. The chart shows the mass of the sponge when it is dry and its mass after being placed in water for one minute.

Type of sponge	Dry mass	Wet mass
Kitchen sponge	25 g	58 g
Bathroom sponge	45 g	75 g
Natural sponge	12 g	24 g
Mop sponge	20 g	75 g

Which sponge soaks up the most water? Explain.

....

....

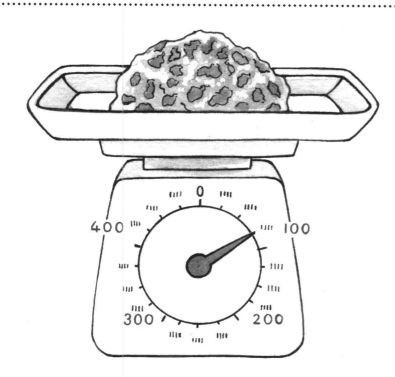

Science investigation

Design and conduct an experiment to determine which paper towel is the most absorbent. Have an adult help you obtain samples of different types of paper towels.

It's electric!

Background knowledge
When you build an *electric circuit*, all of the parts of the circuit must be connected. Each part must also let electricity flow through it before the circuit will work. A working circuit can light a bulb or ring a bell, for example. Materials that allow electricity to flow through it are called *electrical conductors*. Materials that block the flow of electricity are called *electrical insulators*. See website **48-1**.

Science activity
Which of the following objects will make the buzzer sound when they are connected to the alligator clips in the circuit? Place a check mark (✔) beside each one that makes the buzzer sound.

- ☐ PVC-coated wire not stripped at the end
- ☐ PVC-coated wire stripped at the end
- ☐ Spaghetti
- ☐ String
- ☐ Nylon fishing line
- ☐ Iron wire
- ☐ Paper drinking straw
- ☐ Wooden rod

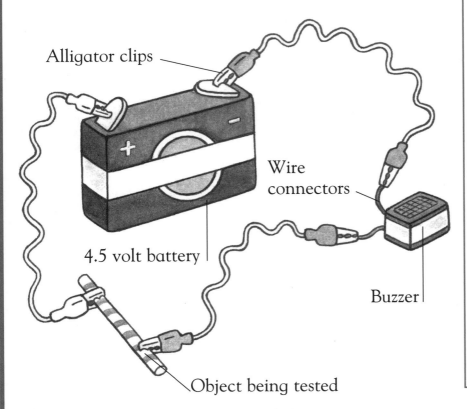

Alligator clips

4.5 volt battery

Wire connectors

Buzzer

Object being tested

Science investigation

(!) Build your own circuit with alligator clip wires, a 6 volt battery, a switch, and an object that will use electricity, such as a bulb, buzzer, or bell. On website **48-2** you can build a virtual circuit.

How hard is it?

Background knowledge

Minerals are natural materials found on our planet. Scientists classify these materials according to how hard they are. They use a scale that compares the hardness of 10 different minerals, each numbered from 1 to 10. The lower the number, the softer the mineral. Talc is the softest, while diamond is the hardest. Each mineral on the scale is able to scratch a mineral with a lower number rating. For example, calcite can scratch gypsum but gypsum cannot scratch calcite. All solids can be given a hardness rating by comparing them to the minerals on the *hardness scale*.

Science activity

Use the hardness scale below to answer the questions.

1. Talc   6. Feldspar

2. Gypsum   7. Quartz

3. Calcite   8. Topaz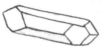

4. Fluorite   9. Corundum

5. Apatite   10. Diamond

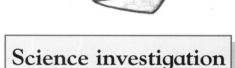

Your fingernail is 2.5 on the hardness scale. Which minerals will your fingernail scratch? Explain.

....

....

A steak knife is 5.5 on the hardness scale. Which minerals will scratch the steak knife? Explain.

....

....

....

Science investigation

Gather small objects in your home that can be scratched. Design and conduct an experiment to arrange the objects in order of their hardness, based on their ability to be scratched by a steel nail or the graphite tip of a pencil. Ask an adult to help you. Do the activity on website **49-1**.

A rocky story

Background knowledge

Rocks are often hard materials. They are composed of one or more minerals, many of which can be seen in a rock's crystal shape or color. Gems, such as diamonds and rubies, are mined from rocks. Metals are mined from rocks called *ores*. Some rocks, such as sandstone, show evidence of living things that lived millions of years ago. These rocks contain *fossils*. The fossil can be an impression of all or part of a living thing. For example, some rocks have fossils, which show the footprints of dinosaurs that lived over 65 million years ago!

Science activity

Use this yes/no key to find the names of the rocks in the pictures.

Clue 1   Are there fossils in the rock? If yes, it is limestone.
          If there are no fossils to be seen, go to clue 2.
Clue 2   If there are crystals in the rock, go to clue 3.
          If there are no crystals in the rock, it is sandstone.
Clue 3   Are the crystals big? If yes, it is calcite.
          Are the crystals small? If yes, it is granite.

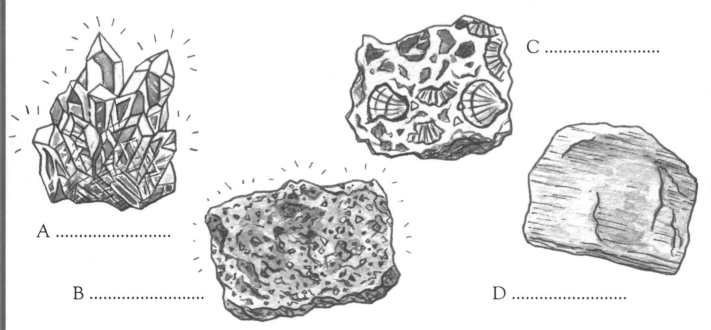

A ....

B ....

C ....

D ....

Science investigation

Collect samples of different rocks and create your own classification system. Place them into groups based on your system. Go to website **50-1** to learn more about rocks, minerals, and fossils. Website **50-2** will help you identify rocks. Try the activity on website **50-3**.

Soil is a dirty business

Background knowledge

Soil is made up of small pieces of rock particles. Tiny rock particles form mud when water is added to the soil. Soil can contain larger particles, such as sand grains. Soil often contains the leaves and roots of dead plants. These dead plants add important nutrients to the soil that help new plants grow.

Science activity

Michiko dug some soil from her garden and put it into a plastic bottle with some water. After placing a lid on the bottle, she shook it very hard until is was a muddy mixture, as shown in picture A. She left it for one hour and then came back to look at it again. Picture B shows what she saw.

A

B

Bottle of shaken mud and water

Bottle after being left to stand for 1 hour

Science investigation

(!) Look at a sample of soil with a magnifying glass. Record all of your observations. Note down if you find living creatures, dead plants, or anything else. Be sure to wear rubber gloves when you handle soil! Go to websites **51-1** and **50-3** to learn more.

Explain what happened.

....

....

....

Does your soil get soggy?

Background knowledge

Different types of soil contain different sizes of rock particles. Soil with very fine particles is called *silt* or *clay*. Sandy soils contain particles that are slightly larger. Some soils contain lots of stones. Most soil is a mixture of all these different-sized particles. The more sand and stones the soil contains, the easier it is for water to pass through the soil.

Science activity

Payal and Demetrius set up an experiment to find out which type of soil let the most water pass through it. One bottle held sandy soil, one held silt and clay, and one held a mixture of silt, clay, and sand. The same amount of water was poured into each bottle. Holes at the bottom of each bottle let water passing through the soil drain into a beaker underneath. This is how the bottles looked after 30 minutes.

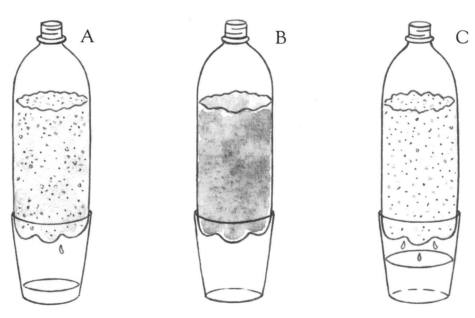

Which bottle contained the sandy soil? Explain. ....

....

Science investigation

(!) Obtain some potting soil, sand, small aquarium gravel, and soil from outdoors. Design and conduct an experiment to see which type of soil holds water the best. You might have an adult cut the top one-third off a liter soda bottle, place a coffee filter in it, and turn that upside down into the bottom of the bottle. Use this filter to test the soil samples.

Keep the wet out

Background knowledge

Many different materials are used to build houses. Slate is a hard rock that splits easily into thin sheets. Bricks and tiles are made from clay that is baked in a kiln. Glass, made from sand, is used for windowpanes. Window frames and doors are made of wood or plastic. Building materials need to be *waterproof* to stop water coming through the roof, walls, windows, and floors.

Science activity

Jamal and Chessie stood pieces of different materials in bowls of water to find out which ones were waterproof. After a few days, they looked to see how far the water had risen up each sample. Here are the results.

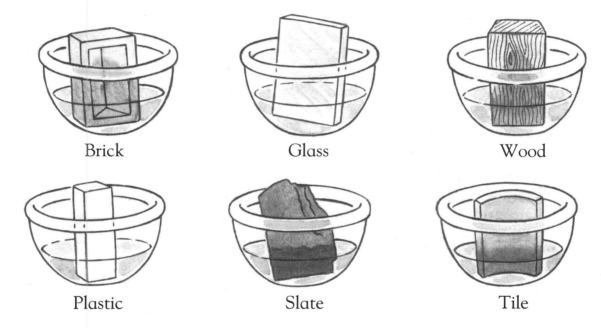

Brick   Glass   Wood

Plastic   Slate   Tile

Which materials are the most waterproof? Explain. ....

....

Which materials are the least waterproof? Explain. ....

....

Science investigation

Design and conduct an experiment to decide what type of fabric should be used to make a raincoat, or to see which of your family's raincoats keeps the rain off the best. Ask an adult to help you obtain samples of fabrics, or to use the family raincoats.

Solid stuff

Background knowledge

Materials exist naturally on our planet as a *solid*, liquid, or gas. Solids have certain properties. They tend to keep their shape. Solids do not change shape by themselves. Some solids can change their shape if a force is applied tn them, such as clay. Solids cannot be poured. They do not spread out or fill a bottle.

Science activity

Look at the materials below. Put a check mark (✔) by each material you think is a solid. *Hint*: For materials such as sand and salt, think about the individual grains.

Modeling clay ☐

Aluminium kitchen foil ☐

Wood ☐

Sand ☐

Salt ☐

Marbles ☐

Science investigation

(!) Collect some solid materials from your home. Look over your materials and decide how they are alike and how they differ. Organize your observations into a chart. Are there any samples difficult to classify as a solid? Explain. What do you conclude about solid materials? Go to websites **54-1** and **54-2** to learn more.

Runny materials

Background knowledge

Liquids are materials that make things wet. All liquids flow. This means that they are runny and you can pour them. If you spill liquids, they spread out. If you pour a liquid into a container, it takes the shape of the container. If you leave a liquid to stand, its surface will flatten, with the edges a bit higher than the center. You can easily push your finger through a liquid.

Science activity

Lauren and Tai did an experiment to find out which of the five liquids below was the runniest. The same amount of each liquid was poured from a pitcher into a glass. Each pitcher was held in the same position over the glass. The time it took to fill each glass was written down.

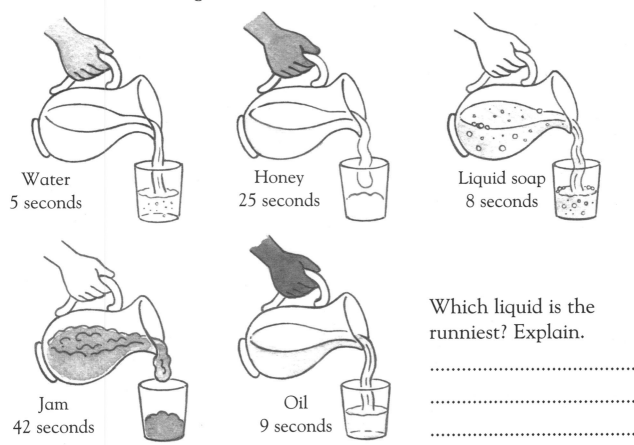

Water
5 seconds

Honey
25 seconds

Liquid soap
8 seconds

Jam
42 seconds

Oil
9 seconds

Which liquid is the runniest? Explain.

....

....

....

Science investigation

Design and conduct an experiment to see which of the following liquids is runniest: water, juice, maple syrup, soda, and liquid soap. Drop a small object, such as a marble, into each liquid to help you determine this.

It's a gas!

Background knowledge

Gases are usually colorless and invisible to the eye. They spread out to fill a container, pushing against its sides. Balloons inflate because of this. Gases form bubbles when they mix with liquids, as you see in soda pop. The air you breathe is a mixture of gases. It contains mostly oxygen, carbon dioxide, and nitrogen. When you blow through a straw into a drink, bubbles appear because you are forcing gases into it. When the wind blows, you feel the gases in the air pushing against you. Some gases sink in air and some gases float.

Science activity

A scientist filled three balloons with different gases. He tied the ends so the gases would not escape. He held them up and released them all at once. The balloon filled with carbon dioxide fell to the ground quickly. The one filled with helium floated upwards. The one filled with air also fell to the ground.

Helium

Air

Use the words below to fill in the gaps and complete each of the sentences.

Floats   **Sinks**

Carbon dioxide .... in air.

Helium .... in air.

Does an air-filled balloon float or sink in air?

It ....

Carbon dioxide

Science investigation

(!) Obtain an empty liter soda bottle. Pour ¼ cup of white vinegar into the bottle. Next, add one teaspoon of baking soda. Quickly place a balloon over the top of the bottle. Describe and explain what happens. Wear safety glasses for this activity.

Name that material!

Background knowledge

Materials can exist as solids, liquids, and gases. Liquids and gases can easily be poured to fill a space. Liquids can make a surface feel wet. You cannot easily pass your hand through a solid. Many gases have no color. Knowing some of these things can help you identify materials.

Science activity

The table below tells you the properties of four different materials – chlorine, paraffin, mica, and margarine. Use this table to answer the questions.

Material	Chlorine	Paraffin	Mica	Margarine
Can it fill a space?	Yes	Yes	No	No
What color is it?	Yellow	No color	White and silvery	Yellow
Can it be poured?	Yes	Yes	No	No
Can you put your finger through it?	Yes	Yes	No	Yes
Can it make a piece of paper wet?	No	Yes	No	Yes

Which materials are solids? ....

Which materials are liquids? ....

Which materials are gases? ....

Science investigation

Using a pipette, place one drop of each of the following liquids onto wax paper: soapy water, fresh water, oil, rubbing alcohol. Have an adult help you. Can the shape of a drop of the liquid be used to identify the liquid? Explain.

This is dangerous!

Background knowledge

In a science laboratory or any factory that uses chemicals, there are many materials that have dangerous properties. Materials that can poison you are *toxic*. Materials that can burn your skin are *corrosive*. If a material catches fire easily, it is *flammable*. Some materials are *explosive*, as they can suddenly produce a large amount of gas and heat. Go to website **58-1** to learn about maintaining a safe working laboratory.

Science activity

Special signs or logos in laboratories and factories warn workers which materials are dangerous. Draw a line from each danger to its warning sign.

Explosive

Toxic

Corrosive

Flammable

No smoking

Harmful

Science investigation

Design your own safety symbols or logos for the dangers listed above. See if others can figure out what your symbols mean. You can use colors or black and white symbols. Websites **58-2** and **58-3** include fun activities for learning about safety. Learn about chemicals in your home on website **58-4**.

All mixed up!

Background knowledge

When solids are added to some liquids, the solid dissolves into very tiny particles and seems to disappear. A mixture in which one material dissolves in another is called a *solution*. When you add sugar to a cup of tea, the sugar dissolves in the tea to form a solution. Some solids will not dissolve in liquids. For example, flour will not dissolve in water. Materials that dissolve in liquids are called *soluble*. Materials that do not dissolve in liquids are called *insoluble*. Water is a liquid that can dissolve many types of materials.

Science activity

Read the sentences below and decide which ones are true and which ones are false. Circle the right answers.

Sand dissolves in boiling water.   True   False

Sugar dissolves in lemon juice.   True   False

Soil dissolves in water.   True   False

Salt dissolves in tomato soup.   True   False

Sugar dissolves in sand.   True   False

Oil is soluble in vinegar.   True   False

Boiling water

Sand

Science investigation

Design and conduct an experiment to see if a sugar cube dissolves faster in hot water or cold water. Go to website **59-1** to find more fun activities about solutions.

"I'm melting!"

Background knowledge

In *The Wizard of Oz*, the Wicked Witch of the West thinks she is melting, but in fact she dissolves. *Dissolving* is when a solid is added to a liquid and seems to disappear. *Melting* is when the same material changes from a solid to a liquid. Ice can melt. When it melts it turns into liquid water, but it is still water. It still has all of the properties of water. When something begins to melt, it feels soft. This is because the particles that make up the material are spreading out.

Science activity

Use the words below to fill in the sentences.

Dissolved   Melted

The chocolate felt mushy. It ....

The sugar seemed to disappear in the water. It ....

The salt and water mixed together. They ....

The popsicle got slushy. It ....

Science investigation

(!) Design and conduct an experiment to see if an ice cube melts faster in hot water or in cold water. Try the same experiment with a piece of chocolate. Do the activity on website **60-1**, but only add heat. Learn about the evaporation of water on website **60-2**.

This is cool!

Background knowledge

Materials change when they are cooled. For example, water (a liquid) changes into ice (a solid). This change is called *freezing*. Food becomes very hard when it is placed in the freezer because the water in the food freezes. Water vapor (a gas) turns into liquid water when it cools. This is the steam you see coming out of a boiling pot of water. Windows may look foggy in the wintertime because of water vapor condensing on the cold window. *Condensing* materials are changing from a gas to a liquid.

Science activity

Look at the picture below. Can you spot five examples of materials that have changed as they cooled? Draw a circle round each one.

Jell-O

Science investigation

(!) Design and conduct an experiment to see whether hot or cold water freezes faster. Repeat this experiment and see whether salt or plain water freezes first. Don't forget to make your hypothesis first. See what happens when you cool down things on website **60-1**.

Is it hot?

Background knowledge

Thermometers are used to measure how hot things are. The hotness of an object is called its temperature. Many thermometers measure temperature in units called Celsius. Scientists use Celsius thermometers. The temperature of an object is written in degrees Celsius using the symbol °C. Water freezes at 0°C and boils at 100°C. Your body's normal temperature is 37°C

Science activity

Write the correct temperatures underneath each thermometer.

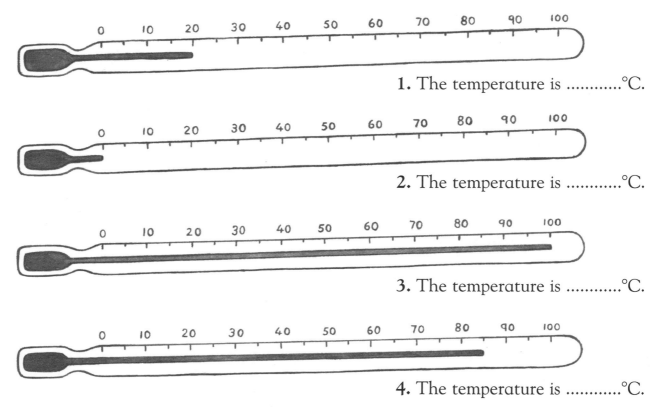

1. The temperature is ....°C.

2. The temperature is ....°C.

3. The temperature is ....°C.

4. The temperature is ....°C.

Which thermometer shows the temperature at which water freezes? ....

Which thermometer shows the temperature at which water boils? ....

Science investigation

Use a Celsius thermometer to take the temperature of the different rooms in your home. Take the temperature in the same room in different places. Does the temperature vary? Organize your information in a data table. What can you conclude about the temperature in your home? Do the activities on website **62-1**.

In reverse

Background knowledge

When ice is heated, it changes into liquid water. If you then freeze the water, it changes back into ice. Since the change can go either way, it is called a *reversible change*. When you heat soft clay in a kiln, it becomes very hard. But when the clay cools down, it does not become soft again. This change can only go one way, and so is called an *irreversible change*. If you leave playdough out, it is ruined because it will not soften again.

Science activity

Which of these changes are reversible and which are irreversible? In each case, circle the correct answer.

Paper burns to form ashes.
Reversible   Irreversible

Chocolate melts in your hand.
Reversible   Irreversible

Egg whites and sugar
cook to form meringues.
Reversible   Irreversible

Margarine melts when
it is spread on hot toast.
Reversible   Irreversible

Milk goes sour in
hot weather.
Reversible   Irreversible

Science investigation

Have an adult help you prepare some Jell-O. Next design and conduct an experiment to see if the Jell-O is a reversible or irreversible material.

Filter it!

Background knowledge

Sometimes it is necessary to separate a mixture. For example, coffee filters are used to keep the coffee grinds out of the coffee. When you pour coffee into a filter, the holes in the filter are large enough for the water to drain away, but too small for the grinds to pass through. The coffee grinds are trapped by the filter. When the materials in a mixture are *insoluble* in water, you can use a filter to separate them.

Science activity

Here are some lentils, peas, and marbles all mixed up in a pot. Pictures A and B show the bottom of the pot. On A, draw the sizes of the holes you must make to separate the lentils from the peas and marbles. On B, draw the holes you would need to make to separate the lentils and peas from the marbles.

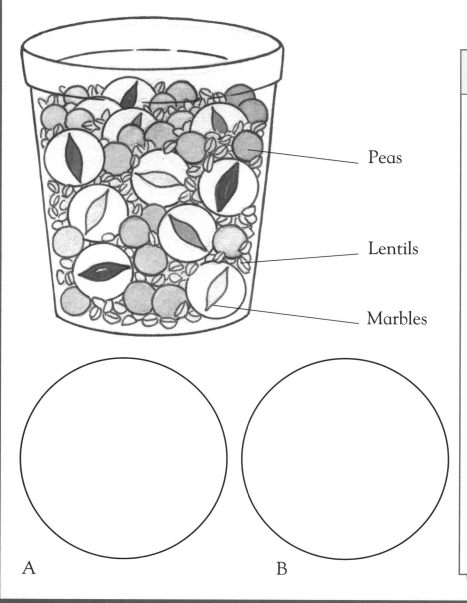

Peas

Lentils

Marbles

A

B

Science investigation

Mix together sand, potting soil, and aquarium gravel. Design a filtering method to separate this mixture. Use your knowledge about the properties of each material in the mixture. Test out your filtering method. Did it work? What are some of the problems you had in your design?

Mix and match

Background knowledge

Mixtures are two or more materials combined together. They can be separated in many different ways. To find out which is the best way to separate a mixture, you must first ask yourself some important questions. For example, are the materials in the mixture soluble? Are the materials attracted to a magnet? Do the materials change when they are heated? What size are the particles in the mixture?

Science activity

On the left, you can see four mixtures. On the right are four different methods for separating mixtures. Draw a line between each mixture and the best separation method. On a separate piece of paper, explain your choice.

Steel nails and copper nails

Dissolve in water and then use a filter.

Use a colander.

Rice and mung beans

Use a magnet.

Science investigation

(!) Suppose somebody mixed together sand, paper clips, and sugar. Design and conduct an experiment that will separate the three materials from one another. How could you get the sugar back if you dissolved it in water? The activity on website **65-1** will help you.

Soil containing mud and sand

Shake in a bottle with some water and leave to settle.

Sand and salt

Can you see the light?

Background knowledge

A bulb will only light up if it is part of an *electric circuit*. A circuit is a complete path around which electricity can flow. It must include a source of electricity, such as a *battery*. To make a circuit, the bulb is connected to the battery by wires. Electricity flows out of the battery, around the circuit, and back into the battery. Electricity always leaves the negative end of a battery and returns to its positive end. The bulb will light up when electricity flows through it.

Science activity

Nina made a bulb light up by connecting these parts together to make an electric circuit. Draw the circuit she made on a separate piece of paper.

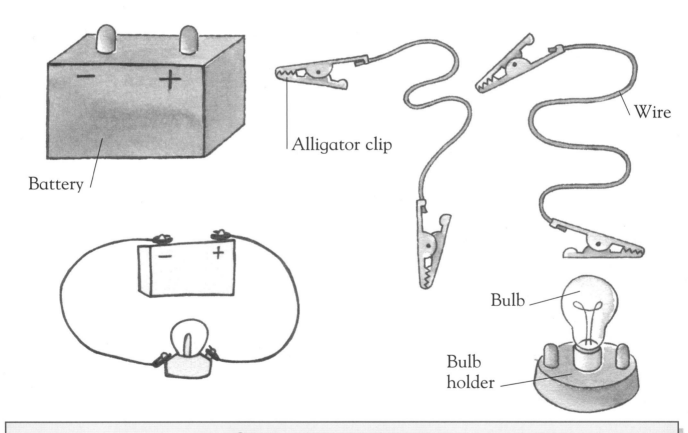

Battery

Alligator clip

Wire

Bulb

Bulb holder

Science investigation

(!) Obtain a 6 volt battery, two small bulbs, and at least three alligator clip wires. Build a circuit first with one bulb, then with two. What happens to the brightness of the light? Go to website **66-1** for more fun with circuits.

Flick the switch

Background knowledge

When you turn on the light in your room, you are using an *electrical switch*. A switch turns a circuit on and off. The switch closes a gap, which completes a circuit so that electricity can flow through it. When the switch is opened, the gap returns and electricity stops flowing. A switch can be placed anywhere on a circuit.

Science activity

On the right is a simple switch. To make it work, push down on the metal strip until it touches the connecting pin to complete the circuit. Look at the circuit diagram below. Is the bulb on or off on each one? Circle the correct answer.

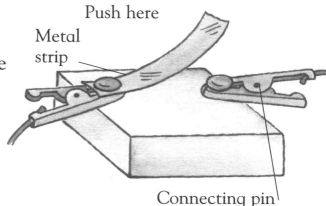

Push here

Metal strip

Connecting pin

Key to diagrams

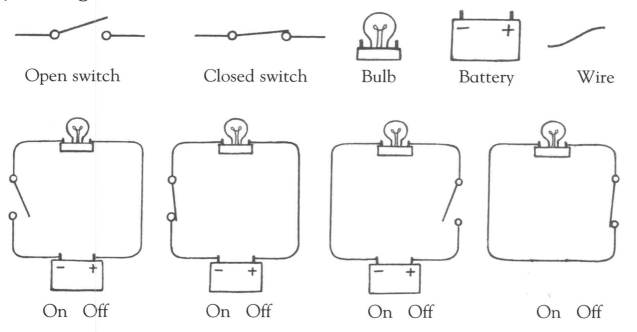

Open switch   Closed switch   Bulb   Battery   Wire

On   Off   On   Off   On   Off   On   Off

Science investigation

(!) Build a circuit using a battery, bulb, and alligator clip wires. Now design your own switch. You might use balsa wood, metal tacks, and heavy-duty aluminum foil. Test out your switch. Go to website **67-1** to learn more.

Magnet magic

Background knowledge

A *magnet* is a type of material that pulls on some metal objects. The magnet is said to *attract* the object. Magnets attract the metals iron, cobalt, nickel, and steel, but they do not attract other metals. Magnets can attract or *repel* (push away) another magnet. The force of a magnet can be felt from a distance. For example, an iron nail placed near a magnet will move toward the magnet. It looks like magic, but it is just the force of magnetism!

Science activity

Draw a line from the magnet to each of the metal objects it will most likely attract.

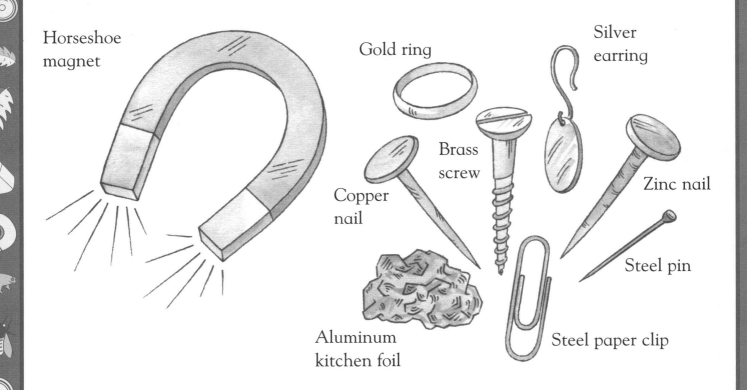

Horseshoe magnet

Gold ring

Silver earring

Copper nail

Brass screw

Zinc nail

Steel pin

Aluminum kitchen foil

Steel paper clip

Science investigation

Test various materials' attraction to a magnet. Note down any samples that were repelled. What happens to the attraction as the magnet is moved away from the object? Do the activity on website **68-1**.

Magnets are forceful

Background knowledge

The most common magnets in a home are used to stick objects to the refrigerator. Magnets come in many different shapes and sizes. For example, some are horseshoe shaped. Others are shaped like rings, bars, discs, and rods. Some magnets pull harder than others. Some special magnets are so strong that they can pick up a car! All magnets can attract things from a distance.

Science activity

Each of the magnets was dipped into a box of steel paper clips. Place a check mark (✔) by the strongest magnet.

Science investigation

Gather some objects made of steel, such as a coat hanger. Obtain a bar magnet and stroke the object in the same direction, making sure to lift the magnet away from the object between strokes. Objects that are attracted to a magnet can be made into temporary magnets. Now design and conduct an experiment to decide which temporary magnet is the strongest.

Attract or repel?

Background knowledge

On every magnet, the *magnetic poles* are where the force of magnetism is strongest. The north pole of one magnet will always attract the south pole of another magnet. If two south poles or two north poles are placed near one another, they will *repel* each other. When two magnets repel, they push away from one another. Earth is a gigantic magnet—it has a magnetic north and south pole.

Science activity

Look at the pairs of magnets in the pictures. Which pairs will attract each other? Which pairs will repel each other? Circle your answers.

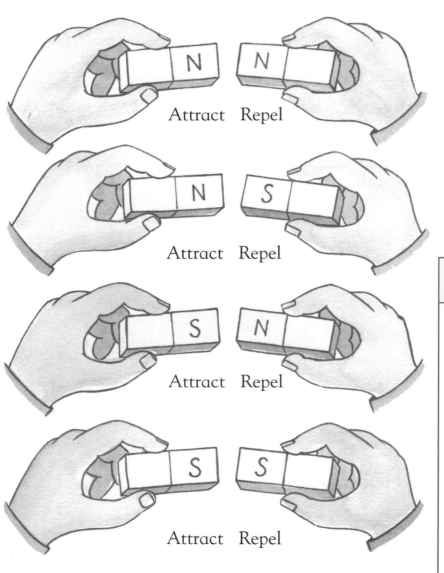

Attract   Repel

Attract   Repel

Attract   Repel

Attract   Repel

Science investigation

Obtain 3–4 lifesaver-shaped magnets, and a dowel or pencil that will fit through the magnets' openings. Place the dowel vertically at a base of styrofoam or balsa wood. Try stacking the magnets in different ways on the dowel. Record and explain all of your observations. Do the activity on website **70-1**.

Pushing and pulling

Background knowledge

Forces can make things move. A *force* is a push or pull on something. *Magnetism* is a force that can push (repel) or pull (attract) things. The force of *gravity* pulls objects toward Earth. When the wind blows, you can feel a breeze as air pushes against you. When you drop a ball, the force of gravity pulls it toward Earth.

Science activity

The pictures show a number of forces in action. Decide whether the force is a push or pull. Write your answer beside each picture.

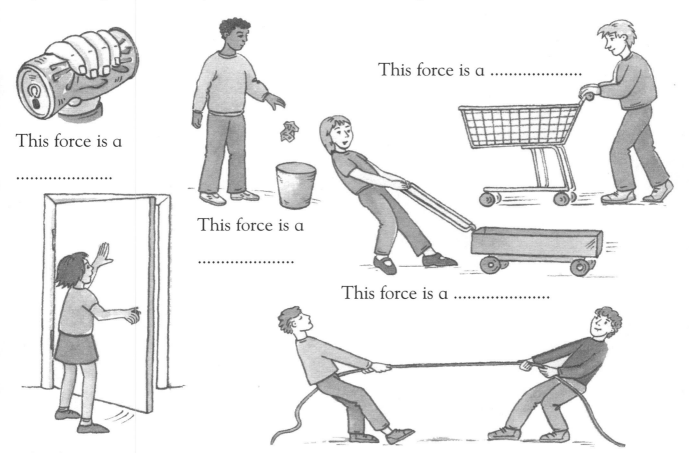

This force is a ....

This force is a ....

This force is a ....

This force is a ....

This force is a ....

This force is a ....

Science investigation

Using a bathroom scale, design and conduct an experiment to see who is the strongest among your family, friends, or classmates. Does a person's size make a difference? Can you push harder with your hand or finger? Does a leg push harder than an arm? Do the activity on website **71-1**.

May the force be with you!

Background knowledge

Forces can make objects at rest begin to move. Forces can also cause moving objects to speed up, slow down, change direction, or stop. Air is a force that pushes against all objects. The pushing force of air is called *air resistance*. A parachute slows down a falling object because of upward-pushing air resistance.

Science activity

Jason and Eduardo were having fun blowing at a ping-pong ball through straws. Draw a line from each picture to the words on the right that explain what will happen to the ping-pong ball.

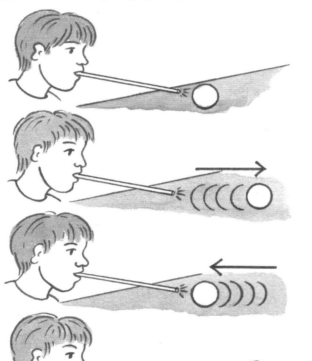

The ball is not moving.

It will speed up.

The ball is rolling away from Jason.

It will slow down.

The ball is rolling toward Jason.

It will start to move.

The ball is rolling across the table.

It will not move.

Eduardo is blowing from the other side, just as hard as Jason.

It will change direction.

Science investigation

Does a large piece of paper or small piece of paper fall first? Design and conduct an experiment to see what effect air resistance has on different-sized pieces of falling paper. Do the activity on website **72-1**.

Friction is forceful

Background knowledge

When you kick a ball, it does not move forever. It gradually slows down and stops. The force that makes the ball slow down is *friction*. Friction is a force that opposes motion. Friction occurs between two surfaces that are touching, such as the surface of the ball and the ground. Some surfaces produce more friction than others.

Science activity

Jamal and Megan rolled marbles down a tube and measured how fast each marble rolled. They tried rolling the marbles over different surfaces. They kept the angle of the tube the same each time. Here are the results.

Surface	Distance marble rolls
Gravel path	21 cm
Grass	3 cm
Kitchen floor	163 cm
Carpet	32 cm
Pavement	85 cm

Which surface produced the most friction?

How was this surface different from the other surfaces?

Science investigation

On which surface does a car travel the fastest? Create three ramps out of cardboard or wood. Cover one ramp with fabric or sandpaper. Cover the second with aluminum foil and the third with a material of your choice. Use a book to make an incline. Obtain a small toy car. Design and conduct an experiment to answer the question. Try the activity on website **73-1**.

In ship shape

Background knowledge

When a boat moves through water, friction between the bottom of the boat (the hull) and the water slows the boat down. This type of friction is called *drag*. Drag pushes opposite to the boat's movement. The shape of a ship affects how well it can move through the water. Streamlined boats move through water more easily because there is less drag on the boat.

Science activity

Jessica and James made three models of sailboats. Each had a different-shaped hull. In order to create wind for the sails, Jessica used a long cardboard tube to blow them along in a bath of water. James timed how long it took each boat to sail the length of the bathtub.

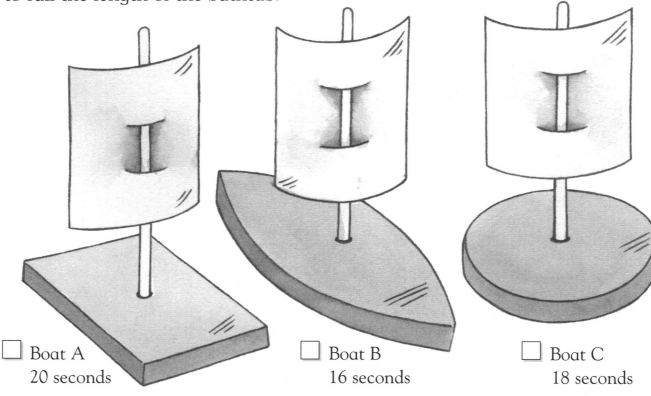

☐ Boat A
20 seconds

☐ Boat B
16 seconds

☐ Boat C
18 seconds

Place a check mark (✔) in the box beside the boat that moved best through the water. Color in the boat with the most streamlined hull.

Science investigation

Try different airplane designs to see which one best reduces drag and creates the most lift. Go to websites **74-1** and **74-2** for design help. Explain how your design reduces drag and creates lift.

Pushy things

Background knowledge

It may seem strange, but when you push on an object, it always pushes back at you. When you walk on the floor, the floor pushes back at your feet. When you blow air into a balloon, the walls of the balloon push the air back toward your mouth. It is hard to push a ball under water because as you push down, the water is pushing up against the ball. Everything gets "pushy" when pushed on!

Science activity

The picture at the right shows where the pushing forces are when you push down on a ruler placed at the edge of a table. Draw arrows on the other pictures to show the direction of the pushing forces on each of the objects shown.

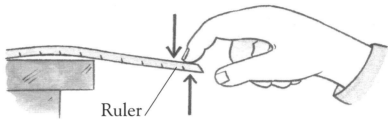

Ruler

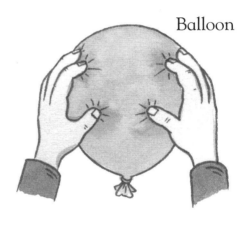

Balloon

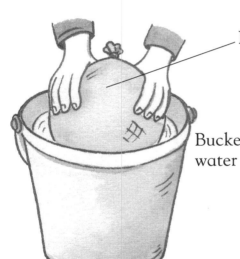

Balloon

Bucket of water

Dishwashing liquid bottle

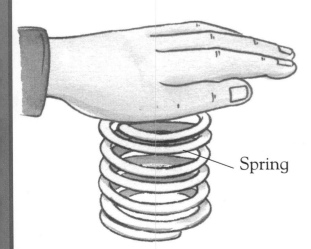

Spring

Science investigation

Push down on a table. How does it feel against your hand as you continue to push? Now find a large rubber band (about 30 cm around). Design and conduct an experiment to see whether heavier objects pull with more force than lighter objects.

See the light!

Background knowledge

The light we see with our eyes comes from objects called *light sources*. Light sources include the Sun, flames from candles and fires, and electric lamps. Some animals can produce their own light, such as fireflies and some animals that live near the bottom of the sea. Light always travels in a straight line from a light source to our eyes. (Never look directly at the Sun, because its bright light can cause harm to your eyes.)

Science activity

The picture on the right shows how light from a fluorescent lamp reaches the eyes of the boy. Draw arrows to show how the light reaches the eyes of the children in the pictures below.

Fluorescent lamp

Flashlight

Firefly

Candle

Light bulb

Science investigation

Draw a picture of people in a room with a number of light sources, including one coming from the ceiling. Now draw lines to show the direction in which light travels to the eyes of each person. If all of the lights went out, would the people be able to see anything? Do the activity on website **76-1**.

The brightest light

Background knowledge

Earth's brightest light source is the *Sun*. The Sun is a star. All stars are composed of gases that are constantly undergoing powerful reactions. When they do, very bright light is produced. There are billions and billions of stars, and even if you counted one star every second for 8 hours a day, after 100 years you would only have counted about a billion! Other stars don't seem as bright as the Sun because they are very far away. Astronomers use numbers called *magnitude numbers* to describe how bright stars look from Earth. Bright stars have low numbers, and faint stars have high numbers. We can see stars with a brightness between magnitudes 1 and 6.

Science activity

Here are some stars with measures of their brightness. Can you place them in order, with the brightest first and the faintest last?

Star	Magnitude
Eri	3.7
Centauri C	11.0
Ross 780	10.2
Procyon A	0.3
Kapteyn's Star	8.8
Sirius B	7.2
Polaris	2.0

Correct order of brightness

1 .... (brightest)

2 ....

3 ....

4 ....

5 ....

6 ....

7 .... (faintest)

Science investigation

(!) Suppose you are a scientist studying three stars of different sizes. Make these "stars" by covering a flashlight with a piece of black paper in which you have made three pinpricks of different sizes. Predict which star will be hardest to see as its distance from you increases. Test this out by having a friend shine the flashlight toward you. As your friend walks away from you, is there a distance from which you can no longer see any of the stars? What do you conclude? Explain.

See-through materials

Background knowledge

Materials that you can see through, such as glass, are called *transparent* materials. They allow light to pass through them. Materials that you cannot see through, such as steel or concrete, are called *opaque*. Light cannot pass through these materials. Some materials allow some light to pass through them, but the objects on the other side do not appear very clear. These materials are called *translucent*. Wax paper is one translucent material.

Science activity

Fill in the missing words in the table.

Material	Can you see through it?	Can you see the flash-light's light through it?	Scientific description
Aluminum kitchen foil	No	....	Opaque
Kitchen film-wrap	Yes	Yes	....
Greaseproof paper	No	Yes	....
Tissue paper	....	....	Translucent
Cardboard	No	No	....
Polythelene bag	....	....	Translucent

Science investigation

⚠ First, design and conduct an experiment to see what happens to the transparency of water when it freezes. Next, design and conduct an experiment to classify materials found around your home as transparent, translucent, or opaque. Use data tables to summarize your findings.

Tracking shadows

Background knowledge

You cannot see through opaque materials because light will not pass through them. When you place an opaque object between a light source and a wall, a dark area called a *shadow* forms on the wall. The shadow forms because the object stops the light from reaching the wall. Remember, light always travels in a straight line.

Science activity

Vimala taped a cardboard circle to a drinking straw. Next, she held the circle in front of a shining flashlight so that a shadow formed on the wall. Draw the shadow that formed on the wall.

Science investigation

Go to website **79-1** and do the activity about shadows.
Now make shadow puppets out of cardboard and
glue them to popsicle sticks or straws.
Write a play for your puppets and put
on a show for your family and friends.
Website **79-2** shows how to make shadow puppets.

Got light!

Background knowledge

Very few things are sources of light, so why do you see them? Though objects are not sources of light, objects can reflect light. When they do, you can see the objects. You see another person because light is reflected off that person. This light travels into your eyes, where an image of the object is formed. But if there were no light sources, you would not be able to see anything. Devices like lamps were invented to be our light sources at nighttime.

Science activity

Jeremy is sitting at a table reading a book. Draw an arrow to show how Jeremy sees the book on the table.

Science investigation

Is it easier to see a silver coin or a copper coin from a long distance? Design and conduct an experiment to see which types of materials are easier to see from a distance. Create a data table to summarize your results.

Sparkle and shine

Background knowledge

Why do some things appear to sparkle while others things do not? Objects that have very smooth surfaces reflect light, which makes them appear shiny. Mirrors reflect light very well. The gems in jewelry sparkle when light is reflected off of them.

Science activity

The picture on the right shows how light reflects off a shiny ring and into the girl's eyes. Use a ruler to draw arrows that show how the light reflects off the shiny things below into the eyes of the children.

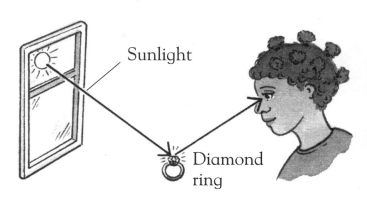

Sunlight

Diamond ring

Moon

Light from the Sun

Light from the Sun

Window

Sunlight

Saucepan

Sunlight

Water

Science investigation

Gather some small objects from around your home. Create your own classification system for these objects based on how shiny they are. For example, you may decide to have three classifications: **not shiny at all**, **somewhat shiny**, and **shiny and sparkling**. What type of materials are the shiniest?

Catch a ray of sunlight

Background knowledge

A mirror has a very shiny surface. Light from a light source reflects off the mirror's surface. The angle at which light hits the mirror is always the same as the angle at which it reflects off of the mirror. Go to website **82-1** to learn more about the behavior of light.

Science activity

Anna used a round mirror to catch the light from the Sun and reflect it onto a fence. On the picture, draw arrows to show how the light reflects off the mirror to form a bright patch on the fence. The arrows should show the incoming light and the reflected light. Use a ruler.

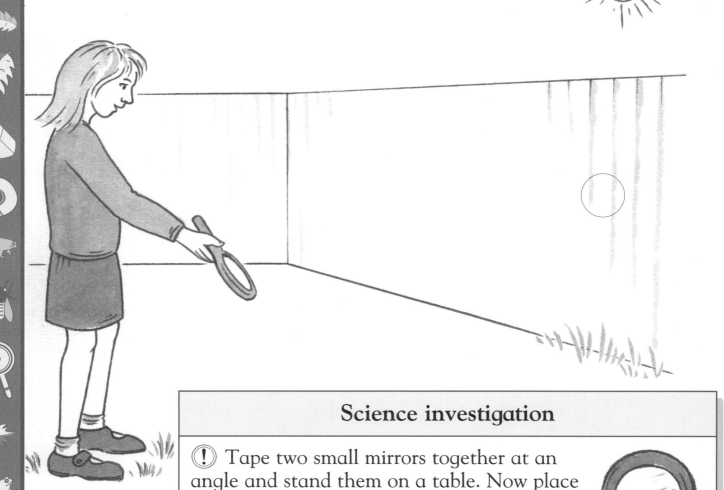

Science investigation

(!) Tape two small mirrors together at an angle and stand them on a table. Now place various objects in front of them. Explain all of your observations. Information about this and other types of kaleidoscopes can be found on websites **82-2** and **82-3**.

Sounds of music

Background knowledge

Sound is made when objects vibrate. We say that an object vibrates when it moves back and forth quickly. All musical instruments have parts that vibrate to make sound. Instruments such as the guitar have strings that vibrate when played, while wind instruments such as the flute have a column of air that vibrates when you blow into them. Some instruments have special parts that vibrate when struck with an object or hand.

Science activity

Place an X on the part of the instrument that vibrates to create a musical sound.

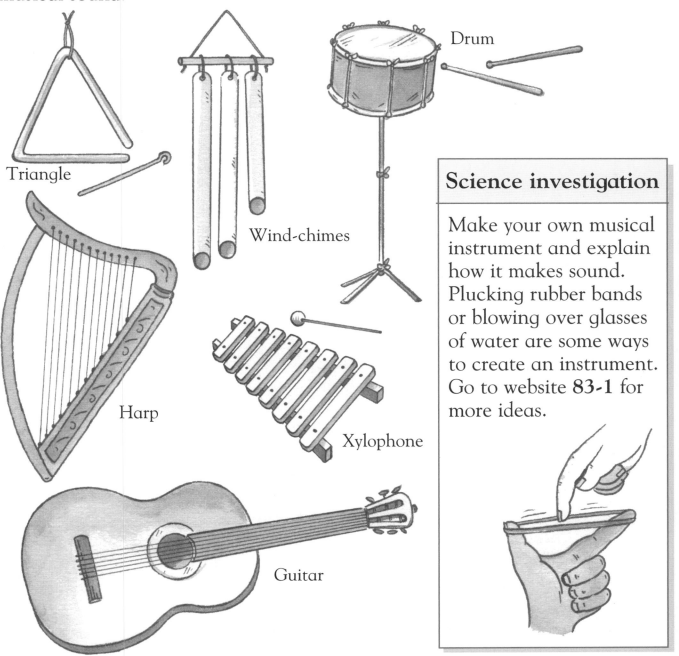

Triangle

Wind-chimes

Drum

Harp

Xylophone

Guitar

Science investigation

Make your own musical instrument and explain how it makes sound. Plucking rubber bands or blowing over glasses of water are some ways to create an instrument. Go to website **83-1** for more ideas.

On pitch

Background knowledge

The faster an object vibrates, the higher the sound it makes. The slower an object vibrates, the lower the sound it makes. How rapidly a guitar string, drum skin, or column of air in a recorder vibrates is called its *pitch*. Pitch is one property of sound. Musical instruments and singing voices can have a high or low pitch.

Science activity

Look at these musical instruments. Draw a line to each instrument to the way you change its pitch.

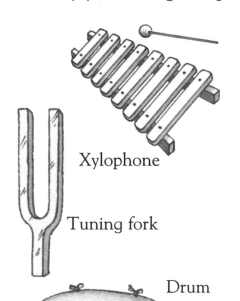

Xylophone

Tuning fork

Drum

Make its strings longer or shorter.

Make the column of air longer or shorter.

Increase or reduce its size.

Change the size of its wooden bars.

Make its skin tighter or slacker.

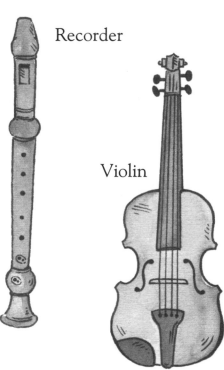

Recorder

Violin

If the air column on the recorder is increased, what will happen to its pitch?

....

Science investigation

Go to website **84-1** and make an instrument out of straws. You will need three straws cut to different lengths, a ruler, and some tape. The straws will be taped together in a row from longest to shortest. If you cannot blow hard enough to make a sound, ask an adult to help you. Answer all of the questions in the web activity.

Good vibrations

Background knowledge

When you blow over the neck of a bottle, the air inside vibrates and makes a sound. The more air there is in the bottle, the slower it vibrates and the lower the pitch of the sound. Adding water to the bottle reduces the amount of air and raises the pitch. The pitch is also higher if you use a smaller bottle, which holds less air. All wind instruments work by making the air inside of them vibrate.

Science activity

Sean made a wind instrument from a drinking straw. He flattened one end of the straw and cut both sides so that it formed a V-shape. When he blew into the cut end of the straw, it vibrated. The vibrations caused the air inside the straw to vibrate and make a sound. See website **85-1**.

What do you think happened to the pitch of the sound when Sean cut the straw in half?

....

Science investigation

(!) Design and conduct an experiment to see if you can play a tune on bottles filled with water. Add a different amount of water to a number of identical bottles. Each bottle should make a sound of a different pitch when you blow over the neck. Adjust the water levels in the bottles until you get sounds you like. If you have any respiratory problem, ask for help from an adult.

Loud or soft?

Background knowledge

In addition to pitch, *loudness* is another property of sound. If you hit a cymbal softly, it makes a soft sound. If you hit it hard, it makes a loud sound. The harder you pluck a guitar string, the louder the sound it makes. The harder you blow a whistle, the louder the sound it makes. All musical instruments work in the same way.

Science activity

Michael put some grains of rice on the skin of a tambourine. When he beat the tambourine, the rice jumped up and down as the skin vibrated. Learn more at website **86-1**.

What do you think will happen to the rice grains if Michael beats the tambourine harder?

....

Science investigation

Make a simple instrument called a kazoo by folding tissue paper over the teeth of a comb. To play the kazoo, you press it to your mouth and hum through it with your lips close together. Design and conduct an experiment to see how you can make the kazoo produce sounds of varying loudness.

Feel the vibrations!

Background knowledge

When a person sings, the vocal cords in the throat make the air vibrate (move back and forth). These vibrations travel through the air to your ears. You hear the vibrating air as sounds. Try feeling the vibrations in your throat when you sing. *Sound* is a type of energy that always travels as vibrations.

Science activity

Here are two children using a string walkie-talkie. The sentences below explain how the boy can hear the girl speak, but they are not in the correct order. Write the numbers 1–5 in the boxes to show what the correct order should be.

☐ The string vibrates.

☐ The vibrations are heard by the ear.

☐ The girl's vocal cords vibrate.

☐ The air vibrates in the girl's container.

☐ The air vibrates in the boy's container.

Science investigation

(!) Make your own walkie-talkie with two plastic cups or soup cans and some string or wire. Ask an adult to punch a hole in the cup or can. Pull the wire or string through the holes and then wrap the ends around small paper clips so they cannot slip back. Design and conduct an experiment to see if a person can hear you through the cup or can. Explain how the sound travels.

Quiet please!

Background knowledge

Sound travels through any material that will vibrate. Some materials, such as metals, vibrate easily and carry sound well. These materials are called *sound conductors*. Other materials, such as rubber, do not vibrate very much and thus do not carry sound as well. These materials are called *sound insulators*.

Science activity

Maria and Brian tested materials to see which was the best sound insulator. One by one, Maria covered her ears with a material and closed her eyes. Brian read out 20 numbers, and Maria called out the numbers she heard. Each time, Brian stood the same distance away and spoke with the same loud voice.

Material	How many numbers Maria heard
Rubber	16
Thick cotton wool	11
Thick wool	12
Thick plastic	17
Polystyrene	12
Hands	10

Which material was the best insulator?

....

Science investigation

Design and conduct an experiment to see what material best blocks the sound of a ticking clock. Place a battery-operated clock with a loud ticking noise in a box. Experiment by placing different materials over the box to see which one can best block the ticking sounds. You could also use a small portable radio or any other device that makes a steady noise. Do the activity on website **88-1**.

A whale of a story

Background knowledge

In air, sound travels more than 300 meters every second (about 750 miles per hour). In water, it travels five times faster, at about 1,500 meters every second. Whales use their vocal cords to make sounds. They also have a very good sense of hearing. The sounds that they make travel for thousands of kilometers through the oceans and can be heard by other whales far away.

Science activity

The figures in the table on the right show how many meters sound travels every second in different materials. Use the information in the table to decide which of the statements below are true and which are false. Place a check mark (✔) beside the statements that you think are true.

Material	Speed of sound (meters per second)
Cold air	330
Warm air	350
Fresh water	1,410
Ocean water	1,540
Steel	5,060
Granite rock	6,000

☐ Whales in the ocean hear sounds more quickly than goldfish in a lake.

☐ It is easier to hear sounds in winter than in summer.

☐ Railway workers hear the horn of an approaching express train before they hear the vibrations it makes in the steel rails.

☐ You hear sounds more quickly in gases than in liquids.

☐ It is possible to hear sounds through rocks.

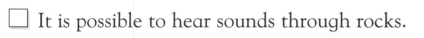

Science investigation

(!) Using two balloons, one filled with water and the other with air, design and conduct an experiment to see if you can hear better through air or water. Make sure the balloons are the same size.

Getting in shape with Earth

Background knowledge

Stars and planets have a round shape called a *sphere*. *Stars* are balls of gases that produce heat and light. Our solar system contains a star called the Sun. Planets are made of rock, gas, and sometimes frozen liquid. Some planets have natural satellites called *moons* that travel around them. Our solar system has nine planets. A satellite is an object that travels around a larger object. Some scientists think there may be a tenth planet.

Science activity

Imagine you are traveling in a spacecraft and are able to look out of the window at out part of the solar system. Which of these pictures would you be most likely to see? Place a check mark (✔)in the right box.

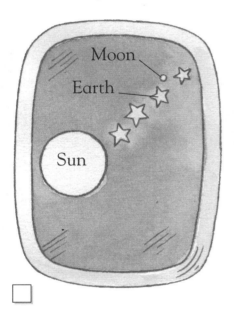

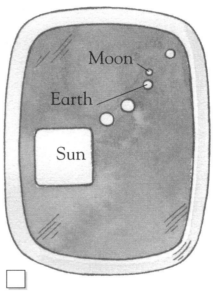

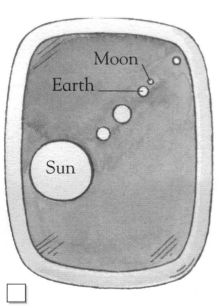

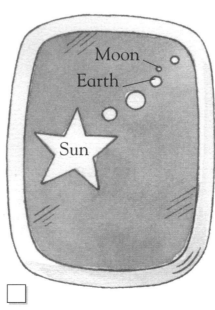

Science investigation

To take a tour of our solar system go to website **90-1**. These other websites are fun to visit: **90-2, 90-3, 90-4** (the last one has a scale model of our solar system and includes information on the possible tenth planet).

Sunrise, sunset

Background knowledge

You have likely noticed that the Sun changes its position in the sky throughout the day. During sunrise it is in one place and at sunset it is located on the opposite side of the sky. The Sun appears to move across the sky during the day, but it is not the Sun that is moving. Our planet does the moving! As Earth turns around, we see the Sun as we pass by it. This motion is why the Sun appears to rise in the east and set in the west. Go to website **91-1** to learn more.

Science activity

Samantha drew a picture of the Sun on a piece of paper. In the morning, she attached the picture to the window over where she could see the Sun shining. (She was careful not to look directly at the Sun.) Draw where you think she had to put the picture in the afternoon.

Science investigation

To watch Earth rotate, go to websites **91-2** and **91-3**. Does Earth rotate clockwise or counterclockwise? Now shine a flashlight on a globe while a friend turns the globe. Describe what you see. How does this demonstration explain night and day?

Me and my shadow

Background knowledge
The Sun is a very powerful light source. When sunlight shines on a wall, it makes the wall bright. If you place a solid, opaque object in front of the wall, the sunlight cannot pass through it and a shadow forms on the wall. Because Earth is rotating, the Sun seems to move across the sky, casting different shadows from morning (sunrise) to evening (sunset).

Science activity
The morning Sun was shining through the window in Tony's home, casting an interesting shadow of a vase on the table. Tony thought it looked great, and wanted to show his father when he came home from work. If there was still sunlight coming through the window in the afternoon, draw how the shadow looked when Tony showed it to his father.

Science investigation

On a sunny day, find your shadow on the ground. Try to change its shape. At what time in the day is your shadow the longest? Go to websites **92-1** and **92-2** to learn more.

Is the Moon out tonight?

Background knowledge

It takes the Moon about 28 days to travel around Earth. It travels around Earth in a counterclockwise direction. It rises and sets during the night, just as the Sun rises and sets during the day. On Earth, the Moon appears to rise in the east and set in the west. Because of the way the Moon moves, we are only able to see one side of it.

Science activity

In this picture, it is evening and a boy and girl are looking at the Moon. Draw where you think they may see the Moon later that night.

Science investigation

(!) Go to website **93-1** to see Moon photography. What are some of the features of the Moon? Does the Moon change shape in the evening sky? Explain. Is there a man on the Moon? Go to website **93-2** to find out. Go to website **93-3** to explore the Moon with the Apollo astronauts.

Day and night

Background knowledge

As Earth spins, it makes one complete turn every 24 hours. Whenever our part of Earth turns to face the Sun, the Sun lights it up, giving us daytime. Whenever Earth turns away from the Sun, sunlight can no longer reach us. It gets dark, giving us nighttime. Day turns to night and night turns to day as Earth constantly spins around.

Science activity

Here is a picture of Earth as it appears from space. Draw an arrow on the picture to show from which direction the Sun is shining on Earth.

Science investigation

Go to website **94-1** and turn Earth to create daytime and nighttime. Go to website **94-2** to see pictures of Earth at nighttime. In your own words, explain why there is daytime and nighttime.

The light of the Moon

Background knowledge

As the Moon travels around Earth, we see different amounts of the Moon lit up by the Sun. This is known as the *phases of the Moon*. When the Moon is lit up and is round, it is called a *full moon*. The amount of the Moon's sunlit side we see, gradually shrinks or wanes. When the Moon is not lit up by the Sun, it is called a *new moon*. During a new moon, you cannot see the Moon in the sky. After a new moon, the amount we can see of the sunlit side grows, or waxes, each night until it is a full moon again.

Science activity

Draw a line from each of the phases below to show its correct position in the sequence from new moon to new moon. (A gibbous phase is when about three-quarters of the Moon is lit up.)

Gibbous waxing   Crescent waxing   Crescent waning   Gibbous waning   Full moon

      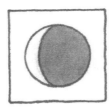   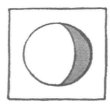   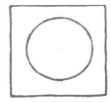

New moon   New moon

Science investigation

What does the Moon look like tonight? What phase is showing? On website **95-1** you will see today's Moon. Make your own chart of the Moon's phases over a month. Go to website **95-2** to see a virtual Moon change phase.

Answer Section
with Notes for Adults
Grades 3-4, Elementary Level

This section provides answers and explanatory notes for all of the science activities and investigations. Ensure that all safety precautions are carefully followed. Be aware of toxic and flammable chemicals. Proceed carefully when using an open flame or heating device.

When appropriate, use the inquiry template to guide the child through the investigations in a manner that parallels how science is done in the real world. The graphic organizer should be used to help the child to better understand scientific concepts while building vocabulary. After publication of this book, it may be possible to download these templates from the DK website. Review the cited websites before the child visits them; in some cases, the adult should guide the child through the website. If a website no longer functions, the DK website may have a replacement link available.

A question of life or death

Background knowledge
All living things carry out certain life activities. They *reproduce*, *grow*, and obtain food or *nutrition*. They all *respire* to obtain energy. Some respire by using gases from the air. All living things must *excrete* or get rid of the waste they produce. Living things also *move*. They may move to get food or run away from an enemy. Last, living things are *sensitive* to the environment around them. For example, some feel pain or heat.

Science activity
The words below describe some of the life activities of living things. Draw a line from each word to the picture that shows it happening.

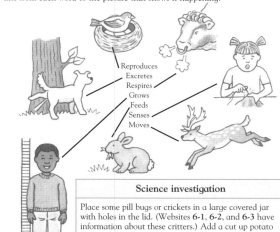

Reproduces
Excretes
Respires
Grows
Feeds
Senses
Moves

Science investigation

Place some pill bugs or crickets in a large covered jar with holes in the lid. (Websites **6-1**, **6-2**, and **6-3** have information about these critters.) Add a cut up potato and some fish food. Observe the critters and note down all of their life activities. Do they engage in every activity? Design and conduct an experiment to determine the critters' sensitivity to their environment.

You might set up two chambers, one with light and one without. These can be made from two margarine tubs connected together, so that the bugs can travel between them. Pill bugs prefer moist, dark environments. Crickets tend to chirp more at higher temperatures.

7

Living it up with plants

Background knowledge
Plants are living things, but they are different from animals. Plants can make their own food inside their leaves. In order to make food, they need sunlight, gas from the air, and water from the soil. Plants use this food to grow and to carry out other life activities. They reproduce to make more plants like themselves. Unlike animals, plants do not move from place to place on their own. Plants are sensitive to light and grow toward it.

Science activity
Here are some observations about an oak tree. Put a check mark (✔) beside any fact that tells you the oak tree is alive.

- ✔ The tree uses its leaves to make food.
- ☐ Birds nest in the branches.
- ✔ It takes in water through its roots.
- ☐ The branches move in the wind.
- ✔ It produces acorns in the autumn.
- ☐ Squirrels eat the acorns.
- ✔ It grows 300 mm each year.

Oak tree

Acorns

Science investigation

Design and conduct an experiment to learn about a plant's life activities. How does it respond to its environment? How do you know it grows? Create your own questions to test. You might grow acorns with help from website **7-1**, or plant red beans as instructed on website **7-2**.

The investigator should notice many characteristics of life as he or she watches a plant grow. If the plant is placed by a window, the child will notice that it bends toward the light, illustrating light sensitivity and demonstrating how plants "move."

8

Staying healthy

Background knowledge
All living things need food and water to stay alive. Foods such as milk, meat, fish, eggs, and nuts contain *proteins* that help you grow. Other foods, such as fruit, bread, and pasta, contain *carbohydrates* that give you energy to move and play. Fats such as oil, butter, and margarine also give you energy. Fruits and vegetables contain important *vitamins* and *minerals* that keep you healthy.

Science activity
Here are some of the foods that Jeremy found in the kitchen. He read the labels to find out which foods contain fats and which contain proteins.

Butter
Margarine
Fats

Cheese
Corned beef
Peanuts
Sardines
Sausages

Proteins

Do any of the foods contain mainly fats? If so, which ones?
Butter and margarine

Do any of the foods contain mainly proteins? If so, which ones?
No

Which foods will help Jeremy to grow?
Cheese, corned beef, peanuts, sardines, and sausages

Science investigation

Play the food pyramid game on website **8-1**. First do the tour, then play the game. Now keep a log of what you eat for one week. Draw pictures of the food and the size of your portions. How healthy is your diet? Could you make it healthier? Website **8-2** has more information on good nutrition.

A balanced diet is very important, particularly for a growing child. The websites in this investigation illustrate the newest food pyramid, which stresses exercise in addition to good nutrition. The sites are sponsored by the U.S. Department of Agriculture.

Munchtime for animals

Background knowledge
Many animals get the proteins, fats, and carbohydrates they need by eating plants. These animals are called *herbivores*. Some animals catch and eat other animals. These meat eaters are called *carnivores*. Carnivores have special features to help them catch and kill their prey. For example, hawks and owls have excellent vision that lets them see their prey from a distance. Go to websites **9-1**, **9-2**, and **9-3** to read more about different types of animals.

Science activity
The animals below are all carnivores. Draw a ring around the parts of each animal that help it catch and kill its prey.

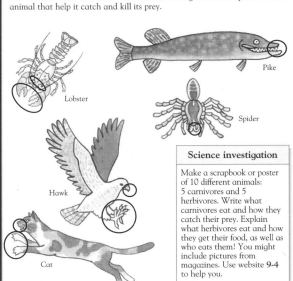

Lobster
Pike
Spider
Hawk
Cat

Science investigation

Make a scrapbook or poster of 10 different animals: 5 carnivores and 5 herbivores. Write what carnivores eat and how they catch their prey. Explain what herbivores eat and how they get their food, as well as who eats them! You might include pictures from magazines. Use website **9-4** to help you.

Most spiders have poor vision and rely on scents and vibrations to locate prey. Herbivores also have features to protect them, such as good eyesight for detecting predators. The websites are excellent resources to learn more about these types of animals.

Rotten teeth

Background knowledge
When we chew food, some of it gets stuck between our teeth. Tiny living things in our mouths, called *bacteria*, attack this food and feed on it themselves. In fact, there are more bacteria in your mouth than there are people on our planet! The bacteria form large colonies on your teeth called *plaque*. As the bacteria feed, they produce acids, which cause decay. By cleaning your teeth after meals, the bits of food are brushed away so the bacteria cannot feed and produce acid. Go to websites **10-1** and **10-2** to learn more.

Science activity
A group of school children were expecting to see the school dentist. Their teacher asked them to do a survey of how often they cleaned their teeth. The block graph below shows the results of their survey.

How often we clean our teeth

Never						
Not very often	Sean	Sam				
Sometimes	James	Amy				
Most days	Oliver	Aziz	Emily	Maria		
Twice each day	Mina	John	Ling	Emma	Earl	Rachel

Which children are most likely to need treatment from the dentist?
Sean and Sam

Science investigation
(!) Ask an adult to help you use *disclosing tablets*, which allow you to see where there are bacteria on your teeth. Now design and conduct an experiment to find the best way to clean your teeth. Find information about disclosing tablets on website **10-3** and try the interactive experiment on website **10-4**.

Disclosing tablets are a good way to test the effectiveness of brushing habits. Using mouthwashes and avoiding sugary foods limit the growth of bacteria in the mouth, while alkaline toothpastes help neutralize the acids that cause decay.

11

Bite on this!

Background knowledge
You have different teeth for doing different jobs. The sharp front teeth, called *incisors*, bite and cut up food. The flat teeth, called *molars*, grind food before it is swallowed. You also have pointed teeth near the front of your mouth that grip and pierce food. These are called *canines*. Animals such as tigers and lions have large canines to catch and kill prey. Go to websites **11-1** and **11-2** to learn more about animal teeth.

Science activity
An animal's skull clearly shows its teeth. Look at the teeth on the rabbit skull and the cat skull below.

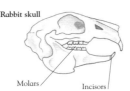
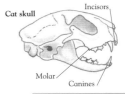

Rabbit skull — Molars, Incisors

Cat skull — Incisors, Molar, Canines

Why does the rabbit have large incisors?
To cut up the grass it eats.

Why doesn't the rabbit have canines?
It does not kill other animals.

How can you tell that the cat catches and eats other animals?
It has large canines.

Why does the cat have such small incisors?
It does not cut up its food.

Science investigation
Go to website **11-3** to compare human teeth with those of other animals. Compare the teeth of herbivores, carnivores, and omnivores on website **11-4**. Now look at your teeth in a mirror. How many of each type of teeth do you have? Are you an omnivore, herbivore, or carnivore?

The child will count 8–12 molars, 8 premolars, 4 canines, and about 8 incisors (some may not have grown or may have been removed). This shows that humans are omnivores, as they have both herbivore and carnivore teeth. The websites reinforce these concepts.

12

The pulse of life

Background knowledge
When your heart beats, it pumps blood to parts of your body through vessels called *arteries* and *veins*. Arteries carry blood away from your heart to the rest of your body, while veins return blood to your heart. Where an artery crosses a bone, you can press a finger against your skin to feel the blood pumping. This is called your pulse. It is a measure of how fast your heart is beating. A child's pulse is usually about 70 to 80 beats per minute.

Science activity
A doctor found that a girl's pulse was 80 beats per minute. After running slowly for 1 minute, her pulse went up to 120 beats per minute. After skipping for another minute, her pulse was 170 beats. After resting for 2 minutes, her pulse was 140 beats.

Using the chart below, draw a bar graph of the results. What effect does exercise have on the girl's pulse?
It makes her pulse go up.

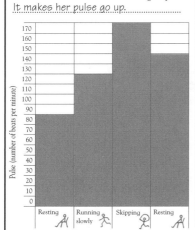

Pulse (number of beats per minute)

170, 160, 150, 140, 130, 120, 110, 100, 90, 80, 70, 60, 50, 40, 30, 20, 10, 0

Resting | Running slowly | Skipping | Resting

Science investigation
Find your pulse by pressing your first two fingers against the underside of your wrist, below the thumb. Now go to website **12-1** to learn how to take and measure your pulse before and after exercise. Design and conduct an experiment to see how your pulse rate changes after exercise. Also try the activity on website **12-2**.

Exercise makes the heart beat faster, providing more oxygen and food to muscles. The pulse rate is the same if felt on different parts of the body, such as the temple and neck. Children with respiratory ailments should be careful when exercising.

Bones provide great support!

Background knowledge
Inside your body is a *skeleton* made of *bones*. Bones mostly contain a material called *calcium*. Your skeleton protects the soft inner parts of your body. *Muscles* pull on parts of the skeleton to make your body move. A *joint* is a place where two bones meet. Some joints allow parts of the skeleton to bend. Your skeleton provides the support you need to give your body a shape – otherwise you would be a ball of jelly! Go to website **13-1** to learn more.

Science activity
Here is a picture of a human skeleton. On the picture draw the four arrows listed below, and label them A, B, C, and D.

Arrow A should point to the part of the skeleton that protects the brain.
Arrow B should point to the joint that allows the leg to bend at the knee.
Arrow C should point to the part that protects the lungs.
Arrow D should point to the part that protects the heart.

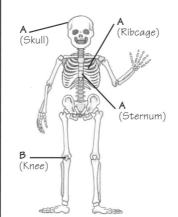

A (Skull), A (Ribcage), A (Sternum), B (Knee)

Science investigation
Trace your hand onto a piece of paper. Feel your bones and see if you can draw a map of the bones on your hand. Go to website **13-2** to put together an interactive skeleton and see if your drawing was correct. Website **13-3** contains craft activities about the human skeleton.

Encourage the child to think about what each part of the skeleton does. The interactive skeleton website is an excellent tool for learning about how they work. Making the pasta skeleton on website **13-3** is another engaging way to make sense of bones.

14 How 'bout them bones!

Background knowledge
Not all animals have bones. Animals with bony skeletons inside of them are called *vertebrates*. All vertebrates have a backbone. Vertebrates include humans, dogs, snakes, fish, and birds. Skeletons give protection and support to the body, and help it to move. Animals such as worms, insects, snails, and jellyfish do not have bony skeletons; they are called *invertebrates*.

Science activity
Here are the skeletons of a fish, a bird, and a frog. On each of the drawings, color in the part that protects the brain, and color in the backbone.

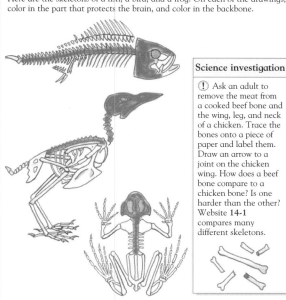

Science investigation

(!) Ask an adult to remove the meat from a cooked beef bone and the wing, leg, and neck of a chicken. Trace the bones onto a piece of paper and label them. Draw an arrow to a joint on the chicken wing. How does a beef bone compare to a chicken bone? Is one harder than the other? Website **14-1** compares many different skeletons.

All animal skeletons protect the soft internal organs, provide anchor points for muscles, and give rigidity and support to the body. Ask the child how joints help an animal move. Website **14-1** compares the motion of different animals. Ants have an exoskeleton.

15 Can you make a muscle? ⭐

Background knowledge
The muscles all over your body move your skeleton. When muscles work, they get thicker and shorter. We say that muscles *contract*. When a person "makes a muscle," you seee their muscle contract. A contracting muscle pulls on a bone, making it move. Muscles need energy to work. They get their energy from sugars in your blood. Most muscles rest or relax after they have been used. They get longer and flatter. The heart is a muscle that works very hard – every time you feel a pulse, your heart muscle has contracted! Go to website **15-1** to learn more.

Science activity
When you move your legs, feet, hands, or arms, the muscles that move them get thicker and shorter.

On picture A, draw arrows pointing to where you think the muscles moving the foot will get thicker.

On picture B, draw an arrow pointing to where you think the muscle raising the forearm will get thicker.

Movement of arm

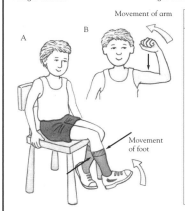

A   B

Movement of foot

Science investigation

Design and conduct an experiment to see how your muscles move your arms and legs. Which muscles thicken and shorten when you move different parts of your body? Go to website **15-2** to learn more about muscles and bones.

Movement of leg

Limbs move when muscles contract. By flexing the lower knee, the child will feel the thigh muscles contract and relax. The websites provide more information, and the interactive one shows how muscles move the leg in the knee joint.

16 ⭐ The good and bad of drugs

Background knowledge
When you are ill, you may need to take medicines to help you get better. A doctor or pharmacist tells you what medicine to take. Medicines contain *drugs*, which have an effect on your body. Some of these drugs may reduce fever, coughing, and sneezing. Others may treat an upset stomach. Alcohol and nicotine in cigarettes are also drugs, but they are not medicines. In fact, they can harm or even kill you. Some drugs, such as heroin, cannabis, and cocaine, are considered so harmful that it is against the law to own or sell them.

Science activity
Which of these drugs would you normally get from a pharmacy or drugstore? Place a check mark (✔) by each one.

Wine ☐

Cough medicine ✔

Indigestion medicine ✔

Beer ☐

Headache pills ✔

Eye drops ✔

Antiseptic cream ✔

Cigarettes ☐

Science investigation

(!) Take the quiz on website **16-1**. Ask an adult to show you the warning on a packet of cigarettes. Is the warning always the same on every brand? Go to website **16-2**. What are the health dangers of smoking? Design your own advertisement to prevent people from smoking.

After comparing the warnings on different cigarette brands, the child should have an understanding of the health hazards associated with smoking. Website **16-1** is a simple quiz an adult should take with the child. Hang up the poster at home or at school.

17 Great to be green ⭐

Background knowledge
Using energy from the Sun, plants take gas from the air and water from the soil to make their food. They make sugar, and store it as starch. Plants need sunlight to make an important green substance called *chlorophyll*. Besides giving plants their color, chlorophyll captures *solar energy* for the plant to make food. Just like you cannot bake a cake without an oven, plants cannot make food without energy from the Sun. Plants absorb water through their roots. The water taken up by the roots contains important minerals that the plant needs to stay healthy.

Science activity
Gus wanted to find the best way to grow watercress. He took three dishes, put cotton wool in each one, and sprinkled watercress seeds over the cotton wool. He placed dishes A and B on a window ledge and dish C in a shoebox. He watered dishes A and C every day, but not dish B. This is how the dishes looked after two weeks. Label each dish A, B, or C to show which is which.

Dish B.....
The seeds have not grown.

Dish C.....
The seedlings have long, weak stems and small, pale-yellow leaves.

Dish A.....
The seedlings have strong stems and large, dark-green leaves.

Science investigation

Design and conduct an experiment to see what effect temperature has on the growth of seeds. Use watercress seeds or bean seeds. Your refrigerator can be used for a cold place. Do the plant growth activity on website **17-1**.

Soak the seeds overnight. Seedlings kept in the dark grow more quickly. The faster growth is an adaptation to "find" light. The plants are not green, since light is needed to make chlorophyll. Most seeds grow more slowly in the cold.

18

Know your roots!

Background knowledge
Plants use their *roots* to hold themselves in the soil. The other main job of a root is to take in water and minerals from the soil. The plant uses the water to make its food. Some roots go down a long way into soil to find water. Other roots spread out widely to use the water around them. The roots of some plants become very thick because the plants store food in the root. When you eat carrots, you are eating one of many tasty and healthy roots.

Science activity
Shawna likes helping her mother in the garden. One of her favorite jobs is pulling weeds. Here are some weeds that she found.

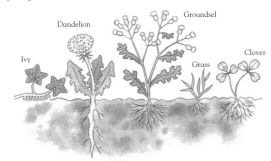

Why is dandelion the hardest to pull up? It has a very long, fat root.
Why is ivy the easiest to pull up? It has very short roots.

Science investigation

Do roots grow up or down? Soak four beans in water overnight. Place wet paper towels around a styrofoam cup. Pin the seeds in different positions on the cup and cover with a see-through plastic bag. Observe and record what happens. See website **18-1**. Do the activity on website **18-2**.

Generally, the longer a plant's roots, the harder it is to pull out of the ground. Carrots and turnips have large fleshy roots called taproots. Roots grow down toward gravity, regardless of how they are placed. Stems grow away from gravity. These responses are called tropisms.

19

Name that leaf

Background knowledge
Leaves are usually green because they have a green chemical inside of them called chlorophyll, which catches sunlight. They also have tiny holes on their surface to let air and water vapor in and out. Leaves use sunlight, air, and water to make food.

Science activity
Use this branching diagram to find out which tree each leaf comes from.

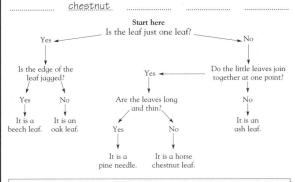

A Beech   B Horse chestnut   C Oak   D Ash   E Pine

Start here
Is the leaf just one leaf?

Yes → Is the edge of the leaf jagged?
  Yes → It is a beech leaf.
  No → It is an oak leaf.

No → Do the little leaves join together at one point?
  Yes → Are the leaves long and thin?
    Yes → It is a pine needle.
    No → It is a horse chestnut leaf.
  No → It is an ash leaf.

Science investigation

 Collect some leaves. Try to choose mostly tree leaves if possible. Create your own way to sort them. Attach each group to a piece of paper and note down how the leaves are similar. Go to websites **19-1** and **19-2** to learn more.

Leaves come in all sorts of different sizes and shapes. They are designed to capture as much light as possible and conserve water loss. This activity will develop the child's skill in sorting and identifying leaves.

20

Flower power

Background knowledge
Most plants produce *seeds* that grow into new plants. All seeds contain a baby plant, stored food, and a protective covering. The seeds of conifer trees grow into woody cones. The seeds of other plants grow inside flowers. Ferns and mosses have neither cones nor flowers. Instead, they have special parts that produce *spores*. The spore cases appear as small specks on the underside of the plant's leaves. Each spore can grow into a new plant.

Science activity
Some of the plants in the pictures below are flowering plants. Circle the flowers. Color the plant that procudes spores (Fern) green, and the plant that produces cones (Cypress) brown.

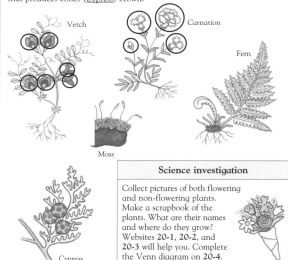

Vetch   Carnation   Fern   Moss   Cypress

Science investigation

Collect pictures of both flowering and non-flowering plants. Make a scrapbook of the plants. What are their names and where do they grow? Websites **20-1**, **20-2**, and **20-3** will help you. Complete the Venn diagram on **20-4**.

The main plant groups are flowering plants, cone-bearing conifers, and spore producing horsetails, ferns, mosses, and club mosses. Fungi produce spores but they are not plants. Collected plants should be dried between a book's pages before being mounted.

Seed detectives

Background knowledge
Seeds *germinate* (sprout) to grow into new plants. Many seeds are formed inside of flowers. Fruits then form around some seeds to protect them. There are many different kinds of fruits, some of which we eat. We eat nuts as well, which are seeds with a hard, woody shell. Some children are allergic to nuts. If they eat nuts they get very sick. Always ask an adult before you eat nuts.

Science activity
Be a seed detective! Which seed comes from which fruit? Draw a line from each fruit to its seed.

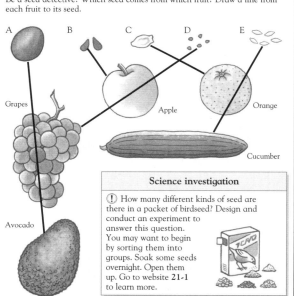

A   B   C   D   E

Grapes   Apple   Orange   Cucumber   Avocado

Science investigation

 How many different kinds of seed are there in a packet of birdseed? Design and conduct an experiment to answer this question. You may want to begin by sorting them into groups. Soak some seeds overnight. Open them up. Go to website **21-1** to learn more.

Have the child decide on criteria to sort the seeds, such as color and size. Encourage the child to plant some of the seeds. Children should not eat the seeds in the bag. All seeds have a seed coat, stored food, and a baby plant (embryo).

Seedy places

Background knowledge

Seeds need to be scattered so that new plants do not crowd around the parent plants. Some seeds are blown by the wind or carried by water. Others are sticky or prickly so that they stick to the fur or feathers of animals, who carry them to a new place. Some fruits burst open and spill out their seeds. Many seeds are inside brightly-colored or sweet fruits that attract animals to eat them. Then, the seeds are excreted by the animals in a different place, where they germinate into a new plant.

Science activity

Here are some seeds and fruits that are scattered by the wind. Use the yes/no key to find the names of the plants from which they come.

Clue 1　Does the seed have a parachute of fine hairs? If yes, go to clue 2.
　　　　Does the seed have a flat wing? If yes, go to clue 3.
Clue 2　Is the seed joined to the parachute by a stalk? If yes, it is a dandelion.
　　　　If the seed is joined directly to the parachute, it is a willow herb.
Clue 3　Does the seed have two wings? If yes, it is a sycamore.
　　　　Does the seed have one wing? If yes, go to clue 4.
Clue 4　Is the seed at the bottom of the wing? If yes, it is an ash.
　　　　Are the seeds above the wing? If yes, it is a lime.

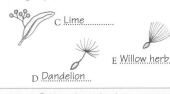

C <u>Lime</u>

A <u>Sycamore</u>

B <u>Ash</u>

D <u>Dandelion</u>

E <u>Willow herb</u>

Science investigation

(!) Does the size of a fruit determine how many seeds are in the fruit? Design and conduct an experiment to answer this question. Use pumpkins if it is fall. Go to website **22-1** to do more pumpkin science.

Help the child follow the key, and decide which clues to choose. The child will need to open a number of fruits to see if size determines the number of seeds. The child should make and explain a prediction before opening the fruit.

23

Needy seeds

Background knowledge

Seeds need water to grow into new plants. Water causes seeds to swell, which cracks their protective coating. This allows the baby plant to get out of the seed. Some seeds need to be kept in a warm place before they will start to grow, while others germinate best if they are kept cool. Seeds do not need to be given food, since there is food stored in them.

Science activity

Here are a number of beans that have been planted in different ways.

Bean A is planted in sand but not watered.

Bean B is planted in soil and watered every day.

Bean C is planted in soil but not watered.

Bean D is planted on cotton wool and watered every day.

Bean E has no soil or water.

Science investigation

Design and conduct an experiment to see if light is needed for the growth of bean seeds. Make sure to use a good sample size of beans. Do the activity on website **23-1** to see what plants need to grow and stay healthy.

Which beans do you think will grow?
<u>Beans B and D</u>

Why did you make this choice?
<u>They are both watered every day.</u>

Seeds need water to grow. They don't need light, because plants have stored food in the seed. The child should place about 10 seeds in the dark and 10 in the light. Control all other factors. Run the experiment for 7 to 8 days.

24

That's my type of animal!

Background knowledge

There are many different types of animals. Some look alike and some look quite different from one another. One way we can group animals is by the features they have in common. For example, animals that are warm blooded, lay eggs, lack teeth, and have feathers on their body and scales on their legs belong to a group of animals called birds. Go to website **24-1** to learn more.

Science activity

What features do the animals in each group have in common? What is the name of each group of animals?

Common features of group A animals:
<u>They have fur or hair.</u>
<u>They feed their young on milk.</u>
....
....
These animals are <u>mammals.</u>

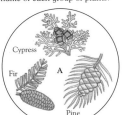

Human　Rabbit
A
Badger　Cow

Snake
Turtle　B
Lizard

Common features of group B animals:
<u>They have scaly skin.</u>
<u>They lay eggs.</u>
....
....
These animals are <u>reptiles.</u>

Science investigation

Place some stuffed animals or animal toys together. Design and conduct an experiment to group them by their features. How many groups did you make? What features did you use? Compare your groups to the groups in the activity above. Visit the electronic zoo on website **24-2**.

If stuffed animals or toys are not readily available, use pictures from a magazine or newspaper. Classifying them will allow the child to appreciate the diversity in the animal kingdom, while learning how scientists classify living things.

Plant groups

Background knowledge

There are many different types of plants. Some look alike and some appear quite different from one another. Plants can be grouped according to the features they have in common. For example, plants that produce spores, contain chlorophyll, lack roots, and have feathery looking leaves are called ferns. Go to website **25-1** to learn more.

Science activity

What features do the plants in each group have in common? What is the name of each group of plants?

Common features of group A plants:
<u>They have cones.</u>
<u>They have straight leaves.</u>
....
These plants are <u>conifers.</u>

Cypress
Fir　A
Pine

Common features of group B plants:
<u>They have flowers.</u>
<u>They have flat, veined leaves.</u>
....
These plants are <u>flowering plants.</u>

B
Daisy　Buttercup
Foxglove

Science investigation

Compare the characteristics of two or more flowers. Use real flowers or pictures of flowers. You might compare the number of petals or color of the flower. Go to website **25-2** to see a flower slide show.

Make sure the child notices flower similarities as well as differences. Comparing flowers will further enhance the child's ability to distinguish between the characteristics of different plants. The flower pictures on website **25-2** can be used in lieu of real flowers.

26

Animal detective

Background knowledge
An animal key helps you to identify different animals. If you don't know an animal's name, a key will give you clues to identify it. Just like a detective uses clues to solve a mystery, you will use clues to identify an unknown animal.

Science activity
Follow this yes/no animal key to find the names of the insects in the pictures.

Clue 1   Does the insect have very large eyes? If yes, go to clue 2.
Does the insect have small eyes? If yes, go to clue 3.

Clue 2   Are the insect's eyes touching? If yes, it is a dragonfly.
If the insect's eyes are not touching, it is a damselfly.

Clue 3   Does the head have a long pointed beak? If yes, it is a scorpion fly.
If the head does not have a pointed beak, go to clue 4.

Clue 4   Does the insect have three tails? If yes, it is a mayfly.
Does the insect have only one tail? If yes, it is a lacewing fly.

This is a damselfly.

This is a lacewing fly.

This is a mayfly.

This is a scorpion fly.

This is a dragonfly.

Science investigation
Click on "sorter 2" to complete the key on website **26-1**. Butterflies are often very attractive insects. Go to website **26-2** and click on your state to learn about the butterflies found where you live. Make a booklet listing 1–2 main features of each butterfly.

The child will need help in using the yes and no key, but will hopefully find it fun. The interactive key on website **26-1** reinforces key-reading skills. Creating a booklet of different butterflies mirrors the careful notes scientists keep when studying a specimen.

27

Plant detective

Background knowledge
By using a plant key, you can become a plant detective and discover the names of different plants. The plant key gives you clues to help identify a plant. The key shown below is a branching key. Each branch asks a question that requires a yes or no answer. As you move through the key, you will discover the name of the plant.

Science activity
Use this branching key to find the names of these fruits.

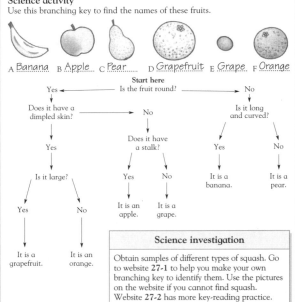

A Banana   B Apple   C Pear   D Grapefruit   E Grape   F Orange

Start here

Is the fruit round?

Yes → Does it have a dimpled skin? → Yes → Is it large? → Yes → It is a grapefruit. / No → It is an orange.
No → Does it have a stalk? → Yes → It is an apple. / No → It is a grape.

No → Is it long and curved? → Yes → It is a banana. / No → It is a pear.

Science investigation
Obtain samples of different types of squash. Go to website **27-1** to help you make your own branching key to identify them. Use the pictures on the website if you cannot find squash. Website **27-2** has more key-reading practice.

A plant key is called a branching, or dichotomous, key since there are two choices at every point. Each question needs to be answered with a yes or no. It may be helpful for the child to develop the squash key with 1–2 peers.

28

Be kind to Mother Nature!

Background knowledge
The activities of humans can affect the lives of plants and animals. *Pollution* from factories and cars can poison the air and water that plants and animals need to survive. See website **28-1** for more information on pollution. When housing developments, roads, and malls are built, there is less open space for wildlife. Plants and animals need room to grow and reproduce. Humans also need to live and work, but there must be a balance between human needs and the needs of plants and animals. Mother Nature is not happy when the balance is disturbed!

Science activity
Draw a circle around each thing in this picture that could cause harm to animals and plants.

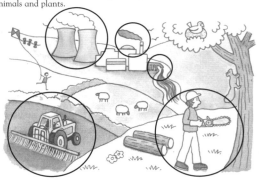

Science investigation
⚠ Learn about local air pollution by attaching some masking tape, sticky side facing the air, to the outside of a window on each side of your house. Leave it there a week. Then use a magnifying glass to look at the tape. Compare it to fresh tape. What can you observe? Explain. Website **28-2** explains how human activity affects the air.

The masking tape experiment will show the child the many "invisible" particles in air. The direction of air currents around a building may affect the number of particles on the tape. Do the activities on websites **28-1** and **28-2** with the child.

Animal homes

Background knowledge
Animals can be found living in almost any place on Earth. The place where an animal normally lives is called its *habitat*. There are many different kinds of habitats, such as in grass, under the ground, in trees, in ponds or rivers, on the seashore, and in the ocean.

Science activity
Where would these animals normally live? Draw a line between each animal and its habitat.

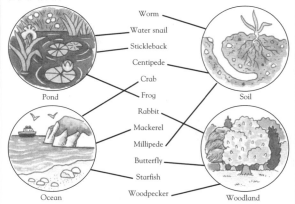

Pond

Worm
Water snail
Stickleback
Centipede
Crab
Frog
Rabbit
Mackerel
Millipede
Butterfly
Starfish
Woodpecker

Soil

Ocean

Woodland

Science investigation
Go to websites **29-1** and **29-2** to learn about types of habitats. Do the activities on the websites **29-3** and **29-4**. Create a poster about one type of habitat. Include the plants and animals that live in the habitat. What type of habitat is it? What is the source of food and shelter for the animals?

Lines in the activity could also be drawn from the soil-dwellers to the woodland. The websites will reinforce the concept of habitats. Although they are artificial environments, aquariums and terrariums are great examples for habitat study.

Animals must fit in

Background knowledge
Animals live in many different habitats. Each animal's body is adapted to
live in a certain habitat. For example, birds that live in water have webbed
feet. Mammals breathe the air with lungs, while fish have gills for breathing
under water. A mole has spade-like feet to help it dig through soil. All
these special features are *adaptations* animals have that help them survive
in their environment.

Science activity
Tadpoles are pond animals that hatch from eggs laid by frogs in the spring.
Three parts of a tadpole's body are named below. In the spaces provided,
write down how you think each part helps the tadpole to live in a pond.

Part of the body	How it helps the tadpole to live in a pond
Gills	The gills help the tadpole to breathe under water.
Tail	The tail helps the tadpole to swim.
Eyes	The eyes help the tadpole to find its food.

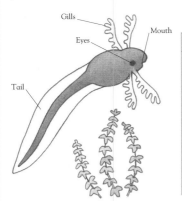

Gills
Mouth
Eyes
Tail

Science investigation

(!) Brine shrimp are
related to shrimp and can
easily be hatched. Their
eggs can be purchased at
a pet store. Hatch some
brine shrimp (see website
30-1), and with the help
of a magnifying glass
describe how they are
adapted to their
environment. Go to
website **30-2** to learn
more about animal
adaptations.

Review how certain body features help an animal
survive in its environment. Brine shrimp are constantly
moving because they are filter feeders. They have 11
pairs of appendages that sweep food into their mouth.
They are adapted to living in very salty water.

31

Dinnertime for animals

Background knowledge
When animals feel hungry, they need to eat. Food provides the animals with
carbohydrates, faats, and proteins, which are important nutrients they need to
grow and live. Some animals have to hunt for their food while other animals
eat mostly plants. Plants can make their own food using sunlight and gases
from the air and water. Animals that eat plants are called *herbivores*. Animals
that eat herbivores are called *carnivores*.

Science activity
Can you spot the herbivores in this group of
animals? Write their names in the box.

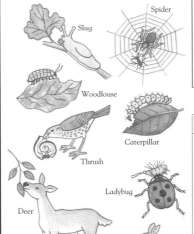

Slug
Spider
Woodlouse
Caterpillar
Thrush
Ladybug
Deer
Rabbit

Herbivores
Slug
Woodlouse
Caterpillar
Deer
Rabbit

Science investigation

Go to website **31-1** to
compare the skull and
teeth of carnivores and
herbivores. How do they
differ? Draw a picture
that compares their
teeth. Make paper
puppets of carnivore and
herbivore dinosaurs
from website **31-2**.
Write and act out a
play that shows how
dinosaurs eat.

The child should understand that all living things
depend on plants, either directly or indirectly. On
website **31-1**, note the particular shape of the teeth
used for tearing meat. The dinosaur activity on **31-2**
develops science concepts as well as language skills.

32

Food chains and webs

Background knowledge
All living things depend on one another for food. Plants make their own food.
Some animals eat plants, and other animals eat animals that eat plants.
Plant-eaters are called herbivores and animal-eaters are called carnivores.
Some animals eat both plants and animals. They are called *omnivores*. The
way in which living things depend on one another for food can be summarized
in a *food chain* or a *food web*. An arrow is drawn to the living thing that is
eaten by another living thing. Do the activity on website **32-1** to learn more.

Science activity
Look at the pictures, and find the animals or plants that complete these
food chains. Write their names in the spaces on the chart.

Plant makes food	Herbivore eats plant	Carnivore eats herbivore
Pansy	Slug	Thrush
Seaweed	Periwinkle	Seagull
Oak leaf	Caterpillar	Robin
Grass	Cow	Human

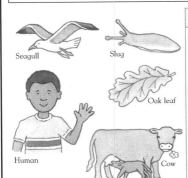

Seagull
Slug
Oak leaf
Human
Cow

Science investigation

Draw a food chain that
shows a plant, an
herbivore, and a carnivore.
Use arrows to point to the
animal doing the eating.
You can use the
information on website
32-2 to help you draw food
chains in certain habitats.

Food chains summarize the eating habits of organisms
in a community. They begin with a plant. Herbivores
eat plants. Carnivores eat herbivores. Third order
consumers eat animals that eat other animals. Food
webs more realistically show eating relationships in
an ecosystem.

Food to die for

Background knowledge
When living things die, other living things feed on them. If they have a
skeleton or shell, it will be the only part left after all the soft parts are eaten.
Earthworms feed on dead plants. Other animals, such as the maggots of flies,
feed on dead animals. There are also tiny living things called *microbes* that
feed on dead plants and animals. Bacteria and some fungi are microbes.
When dead things *decay*, they are really being eaten by microbes!

Science activity
Here are some animals found in woodlands, where there are decaying leaves.
Can you use this yes/no key to find their names?

Clue 1	Does the animal have six legs? If yes, it is a springtail.
	Does the animal have more than six legs? If yes, go to clue 2.
Clue 2	Does it have eight legs? If yes, it is a harvestman.
	Does it have more than eight legs? If yes, go to clue 3.
Clue 3	Does it have a broad, flat body? If yes, it is a woodlouse.
	Does it have a long, thin body? If yes, go to clue 4.
Clue 4	Does each section of the body have two legs? If yes, it is a centipede.
	Does each section of the body have four legs? If yes, it is a millipede.

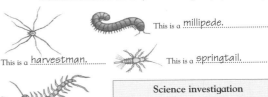

This is a millipede.
This is a harvestman.
This is a springtail.

This is a centipede.

Science investigation

(!) Design and conduct an
experiment to see what factors
in the environment can affect
the decay of an apple core.
Examples of some factors are
temperature, light, and moisture.
Only one factor should be tested
at a time. See website **33-1**.

This is a woodlouse.

Dead animals and plants provide food for a range of
living things. Decay organisms recycle important
nutrients back to the soil and air. They are called
reducers or decomposers. Decay is affected by
temperature, heat, moisture, and oxygen. Website
33-1 can help with composting.

Bad microbes

Background knowledge

Microbes such as viruses, bacteria, and fungi can infect living things and make them sick. They can cause illness and disease in humans. In some cases, the illness can kill people. Our bodies have special cells that fight microbes and help us get better. Medical doctors can give us medicines called *antibiotics* to help our bodies fight some harmful microbes. Antibiotics cannot treat viral infections. Go to website **34-1** to learn more about microbes.

Science activity

Write the letter **M** in the box beside each person infected with a microbe.

Cold M Toothache M Sprained ankle ☐

Chicken pox M Broken arm M

Science investigation

(!) Go to website **34-2** to learn about the importance of washing your hands. Make a poster for your room or classroom about this. Go to website **34-3** and take the hand washing quiz. Try some of the experiments on this website.

Review website **31-2** with the child, so that he or she understands the cause and effect relationship between microbes and disease. The child can place his or her hands in the water with dissolved disclosing tablets to see the bacteria turn red.

35

The good microbes

Background knowledge

Not all microbes are harmful; some are extremely useful. Microbes help the remains of plants and animals to decay. This returns important nutrients to the soil that plants will use to grow. Some microbes are used to make foods such as yogurt and cheese. A microbe called yeast is used to make bread. Yeast is also used to make alcohol. Bacteria convert sugars in some fruit juices to vinegar that is used in salad dressing.

Science activity

Put a check mark (✔) beside the drinks that are made with the help of useful microbes.

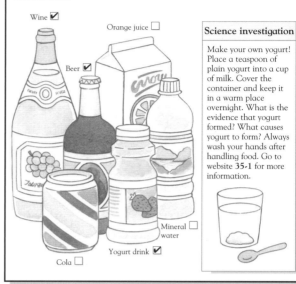

Wine ✔ Orange juice ☐ Beer ✔ Mineral water ☐ Yogurt drink ✔ Cola ☐

Science investigation

Make your own yogurt! Place a teaspoon of plain yogurt into a cup of milk. Cover the container and keep it in a warm place overnight. What is the evidence that yogurt formed? What causes yogurt to form? Always wash your hands after handling food. Go to website **35-1** for more information.

Supervise the making of yogurt. Make sure the child is aware of why the texture of the food has changed. Help the child make a yeast bread to understand how yeast makes bread rise by producing gas.

36

Material things

Background knowledge

Our world is made of many different types of material. Metals come from rocks. Wood comes from trees. Plastic and glass are made in factories. Ceramics are made from mud and clay. Natural fabrics are made from plants or animals, while synthetic fabrics are made in factories. We use all of these materials to build our homes and to make the things we use every day.

Science activity

Anna is blindfolded. Jim is describing four different types of material to her. Anna has to guess what type of material is being described. See how well you can do!

Material one does not feel cold. It is brown. It has a natural smell. When hit with a hammer, it makes a dull thud sound.

The matter is wood.

Material two does not feel cold. It can be almost any color. It has a slight chemical smell. When hit with a hammer, it makes a dull clunk.

The matter is plastic.

Material three feels cold. It is shiny and silver in color. When hit with a hammer, it makes a ringing noise.

The matter is metal.

Material four feels cold and is smooth. You can see through it. It has no smell. When hit by a hammer, it breaks.

The matter is glass.

Science investigation

Write three "clue" descriptions for materials in your home. Hide the materials in a shoebox. Read one clue out loud at a time The person who needs the least number of clues to guess the material wins the game. Do the activity on website **36-1**.

The child should choose a variety of materials that can be safely placed in a shoebox. The materials' properties should be based on what is noted in book activities and the child's other knowledge. An electrical tester can test for conductivity.

A key to trees

Background knowledge

Wood is a natural material. It comes from the trunks and branches of trees. Different trees produce different types of wood. Some woods, such as oak, are very hard. Others, such as balsa, are very soft. Most woods can float, but there are some that can sink, such as ebony. Wood has a distinctive smell. When you hit it with a hammer, it has a distinctive sound.

Science activity

Use this yes/no key to work out which twig is from which tree in the picture shown below. If you answer *no* to a question, move on to the next clue.

Clue 1: Does the twig have a single oval bud at the tip? If yes, it is from the horse chestnut.
Clue 2: Does the twig have black buds? If yes, it is from the ash.
Clue 3: Does the twig have lots of buds at the tip? If yes, it is from the oak.
Clue 4: Does the twig have long, thin buds? If yes, it is from the beech.
Clue 5: Does the twig have one striped bud at the tip? If yes, it is from the plane.

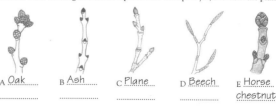

A Oak B Ash C Plane D Beech E Horse chestnut

Science investigation

(!) Collect four samples of different woods that have not been stained or varnished. Place about six drops of blue food coloring into a cup of water. Brush each piece of wood with the mixture. Compare and contrast the way the woods look. Next, after the wood is dry, make an impression of it in rolled-out clay or playdough. Compare and contrast the impressions each wood leaves behind.

Help the child prepare the food coloring mixture. A pastry brush works well for applying it to the wood. Suggest that the child puts on more than one coat. Place the playdough or clay on wax paper and use a rolling pin to flatten it easily.

Metals shine

Background knowledge

There are many different *metals*, but they all have some things in common. All metals look shiny. They all allow electricity to pass through them. They can be pulled into wires. They can be flattened into thin sheets, such as aluminum foil. They feel cool when touched and get very hot when heated. A block of metal will make a ringing sound when hit. Some metals are attracted to magnets.

Science activity

Lindsay and Lisa did some experiments to find out the properties of different objects. They noted down their results in the table below.

Experiment	Object 1	Object 2	Object 3	Object 4	Object 5	Object 6
Is it attracted to a magnet?	Yes	No	No	No	No	No
Can electricity pass through it?	Yes	Yes	Yes	No	No	Yes
Does it feel cold?	Yes	Yes	No	No	No	Yes
Does it look shiny?	Yes	Yes	No	Yes	No	Yes

Write down the numbers of the objects that were made from metal.
1, 2, and 6

Science investigation

(!) Ask an adult to help you build an electrical circuit with a battery, a bulb, and some wires. Cover the battery connection with different materials before connecting it to the wire. Observe if the bulb lights up. Remember, metal allows electricity to pass through it.

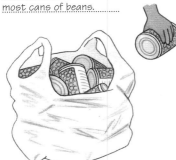

Use wires with alligator clips, since they are easy to attach to the battery's electrodes. Help the young investigator gather samples of materials that have different properties. Parts of old toys can be used for this activity.

39

Are beds made of balsa wood?

Background knowledge

Some woods, such as ebony, are so hard that it is almost impossible to saw or knock a nail into them. Balsa wood is so soft you can easily break it with your fingers. Different woods are used to make different types of furniture, depending on how strong the furniture needs to be. Would you make your bed out of balsa wood?

Science activity

A class of children did a survey of furniture that had been attacked by woodworms. (Woodworms are beetle grubs that eat their way through timber, leaving tiny holes in the wood.) All of the furniture had been stored in the same room. Here are the results of the survey.

Furniture	Number of woodworm holes
Mahogany dressing table	15
Beech chair	20
Pine wardrobe	25
Teak sideboard	6
Oak table	10
Ebony stool	0

Which wood do woodworms find the hardest to bore through?
Ebony

Which is the softest wood?
Pine

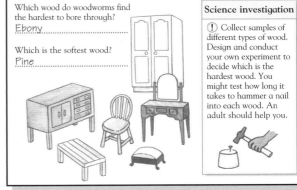

Science investigation

(!) Collect samples of different types of wood. Design and conduct your own experiment to decide which is the hardest wood. You might test how long it takes to hammer a nail into each wood. An adult should help you.

The adult may do the hammering if the child cannot. The child can time or count the number of times the hammer hits the nail. Hit each nail with the same force. Ask the child to discuss possible sources of error in this experiment.

40

Can you bag it?

Background knowledge

Polyethylene is used to make plastic food bags in factories. Some food bags are see-through, so that you can see what is inside them. Others are thicker to protect food in the freezer. Millions of plastic grocery bags are made each day, and most are thrown away after use.

Science activity

Before ordering new grocery bags, a supermarket manager and her staff tested different types of bags to see which one was the strongest. They carefully added cans of beans to each bag until the handles began to tear. Here are their results.

Bag	Number of cans
Type A	23
Type B	20
Type C	40
Type D	12
Type E	20

Which bag do you think they ordered for their store? Explain.
C, because it held the
most cans of beans.

Science investigation

Is a paper bag stronger than a plastic bag? Design and conduct an experiment to answer this question. Use the Internet to see which type of bag is better for the environment.

Use paper and plastic bags from retail stores or markets. The paper bags should be as close in size to the plastic bags as possible to obtain accurate results.

It's flexible!

Background knowledge

Many materials bend when you push or pull on them. Materials that can be bent without breaking are called *flexible materials*. Very flexible materials will return to their original shape. Some materials are more flexible than others. *Rigid materials* do not bend at all, and may break easily if you try to bend them.

Science activity

Samantha and Maayan tested different materials to find out how flexible they were. First the height of each material was measured. Then a heavy object was placed on the material to squash it. After 1 minute, the object was removed. The height of the material was measured again. Here are the results.

Material	First measurement	Second measurement
Cube of Jell-O	3 cm	2.9 cm
Cube of modeling clay	10 cm	3 cm
Bath sponge	10 cm	10 cm
Cotton wool ball	3 cm	1.5 cm
Inflated balloon	20 cm	20 cm

Which is the most flexible material?
Sponge and balloon

Which is the least flexible material?
Modeling clay

Science investigation

(!) Collect samples of materials from around your home. Design and conduct an experiment to rate the flexibility of the samples you have collected. Have an adult help you, and wear safety glasses. Go to website 41-1 to learn more.

An adult should supervise this activity. The child should not bend the material until it breaks, but since this may happen, safety glasses should be worn. They can be purchased at a pharmacy.

Attractive alloys

Background knowledge

An *alloy* is a solid mixture of metals, or of metals and nonmetals. Brass is an alloy of copper and zinc. It is used to make screws that do not rust. Bronze is an alloy of copper and tin. It is used to make bells and statues. Pennies are alloys made mostly of zinc and coated with copper. Nickels are made mostly of copper, and coated with nickel to make them silver. Stainless steel is an alloy of iron and chrome that is strong and slow to rust. Many baseball bats, golf clubs, and tennis rackets are made of alloys, which manufacturers use to make them strong but lightweight.

Science activity

Magnets will attract only the metals iron, nickel, and cobalt. The five objects below are all made from different alloys. Place a check mark (✔) in the box beside each one that you think will be attracted to a magnet.

Brass screw ☐

Penny ☐

Nickel ☐

Bronze bell ✔

Steel scissors ✔

Science investigation

Collect samples of different solid objects. Can you tell by looking at them if they are alloys? Examine each object. Observe the properties of the object and record this information in a data table with three columns. In the first, record the name of the object. In the second, make a check mark if you think it is an alloy. In the third, explain your decision.

The good of wood

Background knowledge

We use a material to do a particular job because of its properties. For example, steel is used to make bridges because it is very strong. Aluminum is used to make foil wrap because it can be hammered into thin sheets. Wood has special properties that suit it to a wide range of jobs. These properties include flexibility, strength, and beauty.

Science activity

Some properties of woods are listed on the left, and some wooden objects are listed on the right. Draw a line to show which wood should be used to make each object.

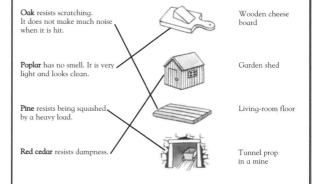

Oak resists scratching. It does not make much noise when it is hit.

Poplar has no smell. It is very light and looks clean.

Pine resists being squashed by a heavy load.

Red cedar resists dampness.

Wooden cheese board

Garden shed

Living-room floor

Tunnel prop in a mine

Science investigation

Paper is made from wood and can be used in many ways. Cardboard is used to make boxes. Paper towels wipe up messes. Collect different types of paper. Design and conduct an experiment to determine their properties. What do you think is the best use of each type? Go to website **43-1** to learn how to make recycled paper. Test your paper's properties.

All-weather gift wrap

Background knowledge

A material that soaks up water is said to be *absorbent*. A material that resists water or keeps water away is said to be *waterproof*. Rain boots are made of a plastic that is waterproof. Tissues are made of absorbent paper.

Science activity

Ling and Tyler wanted to find a material in which to wrap a present that was going to be mailed to a friend in another state. The present was a box of taffy, which would be ruined if it got wet. They needed to use a waterproof wrapping, so they decided to perform a test. First, they stretched five different materials over see-through containers. They then poured an equal amount of water onto each material.

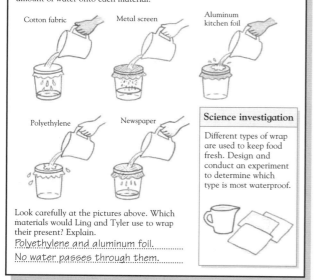

Cotton fabric

Metal screen

Aluminum kitchen foil

Polyethylene

Newspaper

Science investigation

Different types of wrap are used to keep food fresh. Design and conduct an experiment to determine which type is most waterproof.

Look carefully at the pictures above. Which materials would Ling and Tyler use to wrap their present? Explain.

<u>Polyethylene and aluminum foil.</u>
<u>No water passes through them.</u>

Cool and not-so-cool materials

Background knowledge

Some materials, such as metal, feel cold when you touch them because they take heat away from your hand. When heat is taken away from you, you feel cooler. These materials are said to be good *thermal conductors*, as they are able to conduct heat. Other materials, such as wood, do not feel cold to the touch. They do not take heat away from your hand. These materials are *thermal insulators*. They are poor conductors of heat.

Science activity

Five spoons made of different materials were placed in a bowl. Five people each held a spoon while hot water was poured into the bowl. When a spoon became too hot to hold, the holder let go and said, "Now." Here are the results.

Type of spoon	How long it took to say "Now"
Plastic spoon	Did not say "Now"
Steel spoon	15 seconds
Wooden spoon	Did not say "Now"
Porcelain spoon	Did not say "Now"
Aluminium ladle	30 seconds

Science investigation

⚠ Obtain five ice cubes of the same size. Use tongs to handle them so the heat of your hands does not melt them. Wrap each one in a different type of material and then place each ice cube in a small plastic bag. Rank the materials from best to poorest thermal insulator. Go to websites **45-1** and **45-2** to learn more.

Which spoon is the best thermal conductor? Explain.

<u>Steel, because it is too hot to touch</u>
<u>in the shortest amount of time.</u>

How did you get those holes in your jeans?

Background knowledge
Fabrics are used around the house to make clothes, curtains, and towels. Fabrics such as cotton, linen, wool, and silk are made from natural fibers, which come from plants and animals. Fabrics can also be made of plastic, or a mixture of plastic and natural fibers. Fabrics have different properties. Some are tough, while other wear away quickly. Jeans are made of strong fabric, but even jeans get holes in them – usually near your knees!

Science activity
A scientist tested some fabrics to see how well they would stand up to rough wear. She took a piece of each fabric and rubbed it with some sandpaper. She counted how many times it had to be rubbed before the sandpaper made a hole in the fabric. Here is a table of her results.

Fabric	Number of rubs
Cotton	34
Cotton and terylene mixture	45
Pure wool	27
Wool and nylon mixture	30
Silk	12
Corduroy	53
PVC plastic	10

Which is the strongest fabric? Explain. _Corduroy is the strongest fabric. It took the most rubs before a hole formed._

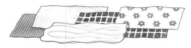

Science investigation
Obtain samples of different sewing threads. Design and conduct and experiment to see which thread is the strongest. Use data tables to record the results of each thread that you test.

Help the young investigator obtain a variety of thread. Use a hole punch to place a hole in the cup, then attach the string. It is important that the string is tied with a strong knot.

47

Sponge it up

Background knowledge
Some materials, such as sponge, absorb water very well. These materials have spaces in which the water can be held. When a sponge is squeezed, the water in its small holes is forced out. There are many different kinds of sponges. Some sponges are natural, such as the sponge animals that live in the ocean. Most sponges purchased for home use are made in a factory. Some types of sponges can hold more water than others.

Science activity
Here are the results of some tests carried out on sponges. The chart shows the mass of the sponge when it is dry and its mass after being placed in water for 1 minute.

Type of sponge	Dry mass	Wet mass
Kitchen sponge	25 g	58 g
Bathroom sponge	45 g	75 g
Natural sponge	12 g	24 g
Mop sponge	20 g	75 g

Which sponge soaks up the most water? Explain. _The mop sponge, because it had the greatest increase in mass._

Science investigation
Design and conduct an experiment to determine which paper towel is the most absorbent. Have an adult help you obtain samples of different types of paper towels.

For the investigation, you could suggest that the young investigator compare store brands of paper towels with commercial brands.

48

It's electric!

Background knowledge
When you build an *electric circuit*, all of the parts of the circuit must be connected. Each part must also let electricity flow through it before the circuit will work. A working circuit can light a bulb or ring a bell, for example. Materials that allow electricity to flow through it are called *electrical conductors*. Materials that block the flow of electricity are called *electrical insulators*. See website **48-1**.

Science activity
Which of the following objects will make the buzzer sound when they are connected to the alligator clips in the circuit? Place a check mark (✔) beside each one that makes the buzzer sound.

- ☐ PVC-coated wire not stripped at the end
- ☑ PVC-coated wire stripped at the end
- ☐ Spaghetti
- ☐ String
- ☐ Nylon fishing line
- ☑ Iron wire
- ☐ Paper drinking straw
- ☐ Wooden rod

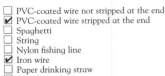

Science investigation
(!) Build your own circuit with alligator clip wires, a 6 volt battery, a switch, and an object that will use electricity, such as a bulb, buzzer, or bell. On website **48-2** you can build a virtual circuit.

Alligator clips
Wire connectors
4.5 volt battery
Buzzer
Object being tested

Make sure that the load (bell, buzzer, bulb, etc.) can take a 6-volt battery. Use alligator clip wires since they are easy to attach to a battery. All of these materials can be purchased at Radio Shack, or a supply company such as Edmond Scientific.

How hard is it?

Background knowledge
Minerals are natural materials found on our planet. Scientists classify these materials according to how hard they are. They use a scale that compares the hardness of 10 different minerals, each numbered from 1 to 10. The lower the number, the softer the mineral. Talc is the softest, while diamond is the hardest. Each mineral on the scale is able to scratch a mineral with a lower number rating. For example, calcite can scratch gypsum but gypsum cannot scratch calcite. All solids can be given a hardness rating by comparing them to the minerals on the *hardness scale*.

Science activity
Use the hardness scale below to answer the questions.

1. Talc   6. Feldspar
2. Gypsum   7. Quartz
3. Calcite   8. Topaz
4. Fluorite   9. Corundum
5. Apatite   10. Diamond

Your fingernail is 2.5 on the hardness scale. Which minerals will your fingernail scratch? Explain. _Talc and gypsum, because they have a lower rating on the hardness scale._

A steak knife is 5.5 on the hardness scale. Which minerals will scratch the steak knife? Explain. _Feldspar, quartz, topaz, corundum, and diamond, because the steak knife has a higher rating on the hardness scale._

Science investigation
Gather small objects in your home that can be scratched. Design and conduct an experiment to arrange the objects in order of their hardness, based on their ability to be scratched by a steel nail or the graphite tip of a pencil. Ask an adult to help you. Do the activity on website **49-1**.

A steel nail is relatively hard, while graphite is soft in comparison. The child can create a new scale based on a scratch test from these materials.

A rocky story

Background knowledge

Rocks are often hard materials. They are composed of one or more minerals, many of which can be seen in a rock's crystal shape or color. Gems, such as diamonds and rubies, are mined from rocks. Metals are mined from rocks called *ores*. Some rocks, such as sandstone, show evidence of living things that lived millions of years ago. These rocks contain *fossils*. The fossil can be an impression of all or part of a living thing. For example, some rocks have fossils, which show the footprints of dinosaurs that lived over 65 million years ago!

Science activity

Use this yes/no key to find the names of the rocks in the pictures.

Clue 1 Are there fossils in the rock? If yes, it is limestone.
        If there are no fossils to be seen, go to clue 2.
Clue 2 If there are crystals in the rock, go to clue 3.
        If there are no crystals in the rock, it is sandstone.
Clue 3 Are the crystals big? If yes, it is calcite.
        Are the crystals small? If yes, it is granite.

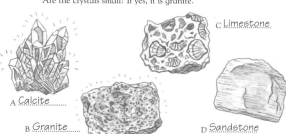

C <u>Limestone</u>
A <u>Calcite</u>
B <u>Granite</u>
D <u>Sandstone</u>

Science investigation

Collect samples of different rocks and create your own classification system. Place them into groups based on your system. Go to website 50-1 to learn more about rocks, minerals, and fossils. Website 50-2 will help you identify rocks. Try the activity on website 50-3.

Obtain some guide books to help the young investigator identify the rocks, or use the helpful websites provided. Two good references are Peterson's *A Field Guide to Rocks and Minerals* and the Golden Guide *Rocks, Gems, and Minerals.*

51

Keep the wet out

Background knowledge

Many different materials are used to build houses. Slate is a hard rock that splits easily into thin sheets. Bricks and tiles are made from clay that is baked in a kiln. Glass, made from sand, is used for windowpanes. Window frames and doors are made of wood or plastic. Building materials need to be *waterproof* to stop water coming through the roof, walls, windows, and floors.

Science activity

Jamal and Chessie stood pieces of different materials in bowls of water to find out which ones were waterproof. After a few days, they looked to see how far the water had risen up each sample. Here are the results.

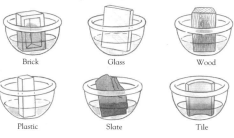

Brick   Glass   Wood

Plastic   Slate   Tile

Which materials are the most waterproof? Explain. <u>Plastic and glass, because they did not absorb any water.</u>

Which materials are the least waterproof? Explain. <u>Brick and wood, because they absorbed the most water.</u>

Science investigation

Design and conduct an experiment to decide what type of fabric should be used to make a raincoat, or to see which of your family's raincoats keeps the rain off the best. Ask an adult to help you obtain samples of fabrics, or to use the family raincoats.

Since there may be small critters in the soil, this investigation should be carefully supervised. Encourage the young investigator to try and identify the creatures, and any other matter he or she discovers.

52

Does your soil get soggy?

Background knowledge

Different types of soil contain different sizes of rock particles. Soil with very fine particles is called *silt* or *clay*. Sandy soils contain particles that are slightly larger. Some soils contain lots of stones. Most soil is a mixture of all these different-sized particles. The more sand and stones the soil contains, the easier it is for water to pass through the soil.

Science activity

Payal and Demetrius set up an experiment to find out which type of soil let the most water pass through it. One bottle held sandy soil, one held silt and clay, and one held a mixture of silt, clay, and sand. The same amount of water was poured into each bottle. Holes at the bottom of each bottle let water passing through the soil drain into a beaker underneath. This is how the bottles looked after 30 minutes.

A   B   C

Which bottle contained the sandy soil? Explain. <u>Bottle C, because the most water passed through the soil.</u>

Science investigation

 Obtain some potting soil, sand, small aquarium gravel, and soil from outdoors. Design and conduct an experiment to see which type of soil holds water the best. You might have an adult cut the top one-third off a liter soda bottle, place a coffee filter in it, and turn that upside down into the bottom of the bottle. Use this filter to test the soil samples.

The larger the particle size of the soil, the more porous it will be. Generally, the most porous soil is gravel, then sand, and finally outdoor and potting soil.

Keep the wet out

Background knowledge

Many different materials are used to build houses. Slate is a hard rock that splits easily into thin sheets. Bricks and tiles are made from clay that is baked in a kiln. Glass, made from sand, is used for windowpanes. Window frames and doors are made of wood or plastic. Building materials need to be *waterproof* to stop water coming through the roof, walls, windows, and floors.

Science activity

Jamal and Chessie stood pieces of different materials in bowls of water to find out which ones were waterproof. After a few days, they looked to see how far the water had risen up each sample. Here are the results.

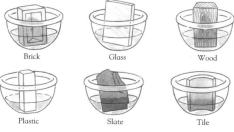

Brick   Glass   Wood

Plastic   Slate   Tile

Which materials are the most waterproof? Explain. <u>Plastic and glass, because they did not absorb any water.</u>

Which materials are the least waterproof? Explain. <u>Brick and wood, because they absorbed the most water.</u>

Science investigation

Design and conduct an experiment to decide what type of fabric should be used to make a raincoat, or to see which of your family's raincoats keeps the rain off the best. Ask an adult to help you obtain samples of fabrics, or to use the family raincoats.

The fabrics that absorb the most water are least waterproof. The child might place the fabric over a waterproof matter and wet the fabric. Not-very-waterproof fabrics will leak onto the waterproof surface.

Solid stuff

Background knowledge
Materials exist naturally on our planet as a *solid*, liquid, or gas. Solids have certain properties. They tend to keep their shape. Solids do not change shape by themselves. Some solids can change their shape if a force is applied tn them, such as clay. Solids cannot be poured. They do not spread out or fill a bottle.

Science activity
Look at the materials below. Put a check mark (✔) by each material you think is a solid. *Hint:* For materials such as sand and salt, think about the individual grains.

Modeling clay ✔

Aluminium kitchen foil ✔

Sand ✔

Salt ✔

Wood ✔

Marbles ✔

Science investigation
(!) Collect some solid materials from your home. Look over your materials and decide how they are alike and how they differ. Organize your observations into a chart. Are there any samples difficult to classify as a solid? Explain. What do you conclude about solid materials? Go to websites **54-1** and **54-2** to learn more.

The young investigator might use clay or play dough, salt, flour, toothpaste, wood, silverware, paper, coins, etc. He or she should notice that some solids are harder than others. Some are flexible and may be difficult to classify.

55

Runny materials

Background knowledge
Liquids are materials that make things wet. All liquids flow. This means that they are runny and you can pour them. If you spill liquids, they spread out. If you pour a liquid into a container, it takes the shape of the container. If you leave a liquid to stand, its surface will flatten, with the edges a bit higher than the center. You can easily push your finger through a liquid.

Science activity
Lauren and Tai did an experiment to find out which of the five liquids below was the runniest. The same amount of each liquid was poured from a pitcher into a glass. Each pitcher was held in the same position over the glass. The time it took to fill each glass was written down.

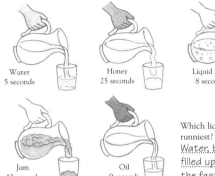

Water
5 seconds

Honey
25 seconds

Liquid soap
8 seconds

Jam
42 seconds

Oil
9 seconds

Which liquid is the runniest? Explain.
Water, because it filled up the glass the fastest.

Science investigation
Design and conduct an experiment to see which of the following liquids is runniest: water, juice, maple syrup, soda, and liquid soap. Drop a small object, such as a marble, into each liquid to help you determine this.

Objects will drop more slowly in the more viscous (thicker) liquids. Use an unbreakable container for this investigation so that none of the liquids leak.

56

It's a gas!

Background knowledge
Gases are usually colorless and invisible to the eye. They spread out to fill a container, pushing against its sides. Balloons inflate because of this. Gases form bubbles when they mix with liquids, as you see in soda pop. The air you breathe is a mixture of gases. It contains mostly oxygen, carbon dioxide, and nitrogen. When you blow through a straw into a drink, bubbles appear because you are forcing gases into it. When the wind blows, you feel the gases in the air pushing against you. Some gases sink in air and some gases float.

Science activity
A scientist filled three balloons with different gases. He tied the ends so the gases would not escape. He held them up and released them all at once. The balloon filled with carbon dioxide fell to the ground quickly. The one filled with helium floated upwards. The one filled with air also fell to the ground.

Helium

Air

Carbon dioxide

Use the words below to fill in the gaps and complete each of the sentences.

Floats   **Sinks**

Carbon dioxide <u>sinks</u> in air.

Helium <u>floats</u> in air.

Does an air-filled balloon float or sink in air?

It <u>sinks</u> .

Science investigation
(!) Obtain an empty liter soda bottle. Pour ¼ cup of white vinegar into the bottle. Next, add one teaspoon of baking soda. Quickly place a balloon over the top of the bottle. Describe and explain what happens. Wear safety glasses for this activity.

The balloon fills with carbon dioxide gas. Baking soda mixed with vinegar causes a chemical reaction and releases a gas. The child should see the balloon inflate, and can press a hand on the balloon to feel the pressure.

Name that material!

Background knowledge
Materials can exist as solids, liquids, and gases. Liquids and gases can easily be poured to fill a space. Liquids can make a surface feel wet. You cannot easily pass your hand through a solid. Many gases have no color. Knowing some of these things can help you identify materials.

Science activity
The table below tells you the properties of four different materials – chlorine, paraffin, mica, and margarine. Use this table to answer the questions.

Material	Chlorine	Paraffin	Mica	Margarine
Can it fill a space?	Yes	Yes	No	No
What color is it?	Yellow	No color	White and silvery	Yellow
Can it be poured?	Yes	Yes	No	No
Can you put your finger through it?	Yes	Yes	No	Yes
Can it make a piece of paper wet?	No	Yes	No	Yes

Which materials are solids? <u>Mica and margarine</u>

Which materials are liquids? <u>Paraffin</u>

Which materials are gases? <u>Chlorine</u>

Science investigation
Using a pipette, place one drop of each of the following liquids onto wax paper: soapy water, fresh water, oil, rubbing alcohol. Have an adult help you. Can the shape of a drop of the liquid be used to identify the liquid? Explain.

All liquids tend to bubble up because of surface tension, an inward pushing force that causes them to form bubbles. The water drop will appear the roundest since it has the most surface tension; then oil, alcohol, and finally soapy water.

This is dangerous!

Background knowledge

In a science laboratory or any factory that uses chemicals, there are many materials that have dangerous properties. Materials that can poison you are *toxic*. Materials that can burn your skin are *corrosive*. If a material catches fire easily, it is *flammable*. Some materials are *explosive*, as they can suddenly produce a large amount of gas and heat. Go to website 58-1 to learn about maintaining a safe working laboratory.

Science activity

Special signs or logos in laboratories and factories warn workers which materials are dangerous. Draw a line from each danger to its warning sign.

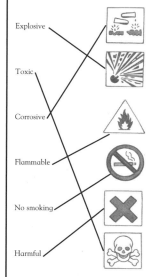

Explosive

Toxic

Corrosive

Flammable

No smoking

Harmful

Science investigation

Design your own safety symbols or logos for the dangers listed above. See if others can figure out what your symbols mean. You can use colors or black and white symbols. Websites 58-2 and 58-3 include fun activities for learning about safety. Learn about chemicals in your home on website 58-4.

The child's challenge is to think up logos that other people will understand without an explanation--for example, logos denoting bathrooms and non-smoking areas. Talk about why these symbols are easy to understand.

59

All mixed up!

Background knowledge

When solids are added to some liquids, the solid dissolves into very tiny particles and seems to disappear. A mixture in which one material dissolves in another is called a *solution*. When you add sugar to a cup of tea, the sugar dissolves in the tea to form a solution. Some solids will not dissolve in liquids. For example, flour will not dissolve in water. Materials that dissolve in liquids are called *soluble*. Materials that do not dissolve in liquids are called *insoluble*. Water is a liquid that can dissolve many types of materials.

Science activity

Read the sentences below and decide which ones are true and which ones are false. Circle the right answers.

Sand dissolves in boiling water.	True (False)
Sugar dissolves in lemon juice.	(True) False
Soil dissolves in water.	(True) False
Salt dissolves in tomato soup.	(True) False
Sugar dissolves in sand.	True (False)
Oil is soluble in vinegar.	True (False)

Science investigation

Design and conduct an experiment to see if a sugar cube dissolves faster in hot water or cold water. Go to website 59-1 to find more fun activities about solutions.

Boiling water

Sand

The sugar cube will dissolve fastest in hot water. The sugar dissolves into particles that are too small to be seen, but we know they are still there because the water tastes sweet.

60

"I'm melting!"

Background knowledge

In *The Wizard of Oz*, the Wicked Witch of the West thinks she is melting, but in fact she dissolves. *Dissolving* is when a solid is added to a liquid and seems to disappear. *Melting* is when the same material changes from a solid to a liquid. Ice can melt. When it melts it turns into liquid water, but it is still water. It still has all of the properties of water. When something begins to melt, it feels soft. This is because the particles that make up the material are spreading out.

Science activity

Use the words below to fill in the sentences.

Dissolved   **Melted**

Sunil: top dotted line needs to be brought down a bit.

The chocolate felt mushy. It ...melted...........

The sugar seemed to disappear in the water. It ...dissolved.....

The salt and water mixed together. They ...dissolved......

The popsicle got slushy. It ...melted...........

Science investigation

(!) Design and conduct an experiment to see if an ice cube melts faster in hot water or in cold water. Try the same experiment with a piece of chocolate. Do the activity on website 60-1, but only add heat. Learn about the evaporation of water on website 60-2.

An ice cube will melt fastest in hot water. Learning science is very observational at this age, so the full explanation may be too conceptual. Try this simplification: "The ice melts faster because the heat in the hot water goes into the ice."

This is cool!

Background knowledge

Materials change when they are cooled. For example, water (a liquid) changes into ice (a solid). This change is called *freezing*. Food becomes very hard when it is placed in the freezer because the water in the food freezes. Water vapor (a gas) turns into liquid water when it cools. This is the steam you see coming out of a boiling pot of water. Windows may look foggy in the wintertime because of water vapor condensing on the cold window. *Condensing* materials are changing from a gas to a liquid.

Science activity

Look at the picture below. Can you spot five examples of materials that have changed as they cooled? Draw a circle round each one.

Jell-O

Science investigation

(!) Design and conduct an experiment to see whether hot or cold water freezes faster. Repeat this experiment and see whether salt or plain water freezes first. Don't forget to make your hypothesis first. See what happens when you cool down things on website 60-1.

Cold water freezes faster than hot water. Learning science is very observational at this age, so the full explanation may be too conceptual. Try this simplification: "Hot water freezes more slowly than cold water because it has to transfer out more heat to freeze."

Is it hot?

Background knowledge

Thermometers are used to measure how hot things are. The hotness of an object is called its temperature. Many thermometers measure temperature in units called Celsius. Scientists use Celsius thermometers. The temperature of an object is written in degrees Celsius using the symbol °C. Water freezes at 0°C and boils at 100°C. Your body's normal temperature is 37°C

Science activity

Write the correct temperatures underneath each thermometer.

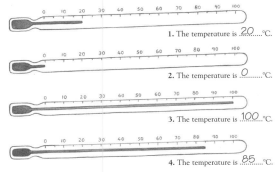

1. The temperature is ..20...°C.

2. The temperature is ..0......°C.

3. The temperature is ..100..°C.

4. The temperature is ..85...°C.

Which thermometer shows the temperature at which water freezes? ..2........

Which thermometer shows the temperature at which water boils? ..3........

Science investigation

Use a Celsius thermometer to take the temperature of the different rooms in your home. Take the temperature in the same room in different places. Does the temperature vary? Organize your information in a data table. What can you conclude about the temperature in your home? Do the activities on website **62-1**.

The temperature in the rooms should vary. Since cold air is denser than warm air, temperature taken by the floor will be lower than the temperature taken closer to the ceiling. Rooms upstairs will tend to be warmer for the same reason.

In reverse

Background knowledge

When ice is heated, it changes into liquid water. If you then freeze the water, it changes back into ice. Since the change can go either way, it is called a *reversible change*. When you heat soft clay in a kiln, it becomes very hard. But when the clay cools down, it does not become soft again. This change can only go one way, and so is called an *irreversible change*. If you leave playdough out, it is ruined because it will not soften again.

Science activity

Which of these changes are reversible and which are irreversible? In each case, circle the correct answer.

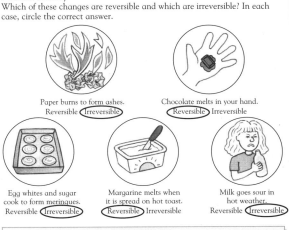

Paper burns to form ashes.
Reversible (Irreversible)

Chocolate melts in your hand.
(Reversible) Irreversible

Egg whites and sugar cook to form meringues.
Reversible (Irreversible)

Margarine melts when it is spread on hot toast.
(Reversible) Irreversible

Milk goes sour in hot weather.
Reversible (Irreversible)

Science investigation

Have an adult help you prepare some Jell-O. Next design and conduct an experiment to see if the Jell-O is a reversible or irreversible material.

Generally, Jell-O is a reversible solid. As it cools, it becomes a solid. When heated, it becomes a liquid again. First let cool it in the fridge to speed solidification. In order to turn back into a liquid, it will need to be heated again.

Filter it!

Background knowledge

Sometimes it is necessary to separate a mixture. For example, coffee filters are used to keep the coffee grinds out of the coffee. When you pour coffee into a filter, the holes in the filter are large enough for the water to drain away, but too small for the grinds to pass through. The coffee grinds are trapped by the filter. When the materials in a mixture are *insoluble* in water, you can use a filter to separate them.

Science activity

Here are some lentils, peas, and marbles all mixed up in a pot. Pictures A and B show the bottom of the pot. On A, draw the sizes of the holes you must make to separate the lentils from the peas and marbles. On B, draw the holes you would need to make to separate the lentils and peas from the marbles.

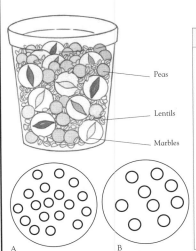

Peas

Lentils

Marbles

A   B

Science investigation

Mix together sand, potting soil, and aquarium gravel. Design a filtering method to separate this mixture. Use your knowledge about the properties of each material in the mixture. Test out your filtering method. Did it work? What are some of the problems you had in your design?

Encourage the child to make a filtering device. Cut holes in old fabric, or use colanders or other draining devices. Emphasize the relationship between the size of the openings in the filter and its ability to separate mixtures of a certain particle size.

Mix and match

Background knowledge

Mixtures are two or more materials combined together. They can be separated in many different ways. To find out which is the best way to separate a mixture, you must first ask yourself some important questions. For example, are the materials in the mixture soluble? Are the materials attracted to a magnet? Do the materials change when they are heated? What size are the particles in the mixture?

Science activity

On the left, you can see four mixtures. On the right are four different methods for separating mixtures. Draw a line between each mixture and the best separation method. On a separate piece of paper, explain your choice.

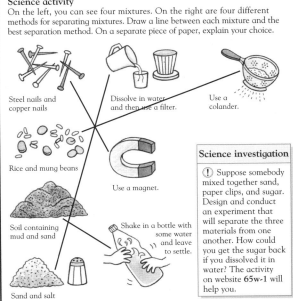

Steel nails and copper nails

Dissolve in water and then use a filter.

Use a colander.

Rice and mung beans

Use a magnet.

Soil containing mud and sand

Shake in a bottle with some water and leave to settle.

Sand and salt

Science investigation

(!) Suppose somebody mixed together sand, paper clips, and sugar. Design and conduct an experiment that will separate the three materials from one another. How could you get the sugar back if you dissolved it in water? The activity on website **65w-1** will help you.

Sugar dissolves in water while sand does not. If water is added to the mixture, the sand can be separated with a coffee filter. The sugar can be separated from the water by boiling off the water—be careful not to burn the sugar.

Can you see the light?

Background knowledge
A bulb will only light up if it is part of an *electric circuit*. A circuit is a complete path around which electricity can flow. It must include a source of electricity, such as a *battery*. To make a circuit, the bulb is connected to the battery by wires. Electricity flows out of the battery, around the circuit, and back into the battery. Electricity always leaves the negative end of a battery and returns to its positive end. The bulb will light up when electricity flows through it.

Science activity
Nina made a bulb light up by connecting these parts together to make an electric circuit. Draw the circuit she made on a separate piece of paper.

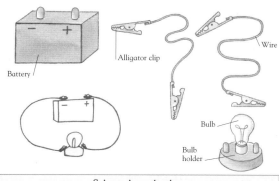

Battery
Alligator clip
Wire
Bulb
Bulb holder

Science investigation

(!) Obtain a 6 volt battery, two small bulbs, and at least three alligator clip wires. Build a circuit first with one bulb, then with two. What happens to the brightness of the light? Go to website **66-1** for more fun with circuits.

A complete circuit is needed before a bulb will light. Adding a second bulb to a three-wire circuit will make the bulbs dimmer (series circuit). If each bulb has its own pathway to the source of electricity (parallel circuit), the bulbs will all burn bright.

Flick the switch

Background knowledge
When you turn on the light in your room, you are using an *electrical switch*. A switch turns a circuit on and off. The switch closes a gap, which completes a circuit so that electricity can flow through it. When the switch is opened, the gap returns and electricity stops flowing. A switch can be placed anywhere on a circuit.

Science activity
On the right is a simple switch. To make it work, <u>push down</u> on the metal strip until it touches the connecting pin to complete the circuit. Look at the circuit diagram below. Is the bulb on or off on each one? Circle the correct answer.

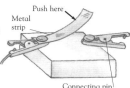

Push here
Metal strip
Connecting pin

Key to diagrams

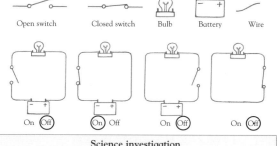

Open switch   Closed switch   Bulb   Battery   Wire

On (Off)   (On) Off   (Off)   On (Off)

Science investigation

(!) Build a circuit using a battery, bulb, and alligator clip wires. Now design your own switch. You might use balsa wood, metal tacks, and heavy-duty aluminum foil. Test out your switch. Go to website **67-1** to learn more.

The child learns how switches are used to control circuits. There are a variety of switch types, including toggle, push, and knife switches. They all work by closing or opening a gap in the circuit to turn it on or off. The website reinforces these concepts.

Magnet magic

Background knowledge
A *magnet* is a type of material that pulls on some metal objects. The magnet is said to *attract* the object. Magnets attract the metals iron, cobalt, nickel, and steel, but they do not attract other metals. Magnets can attract or *repel* (push away) another magnet. The force of a magnet can be felt from a distance. For example, an iron nail placed near a magnet will move toward the magnet. It looks like magic, but it is just the force of magnetism!

Science activity
Draw a line from the magnet to each of the metal objects it will most likely attract.

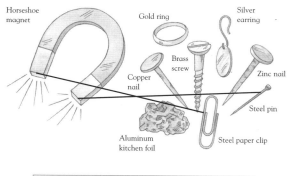

Horseshoe magnet
Gold ring
Silver earring
Brass screw
Copper nail
Zinc nail
Steel pin
Aluminum kitchen foil
Steel paper clip

Science investigation

Test various materials' attraction to a magnet. Note down any samples that were repelled. What happens to the attraction as the magnet is moved away from the object? Do the activity on website **68-1**.

The force a magnet exerts across a distance is called a magnetic field. There is no naturally occurring material that can block a magnetic field. Magnetic fields pass through ferromagnetic materials more easily than paper or wood, for example.

Magnets are forceful

Background knowledge
The most common magnets in a home are used to stick objects to the refrigerator. Magnets come in many different shapes and sizes. For example, some are horseshoe shaped. Others are shaped like rings, bars, discs, and rods. Some magnets pull harder than others. Some special magnets are so strong that they can pick up a car! All magnets can attract things from a distance.

Science activity
Each of the magnets was dipped into a box of steel paper clips. Place a check mark (✔) by the strongest magnet.

Science investigation

Gather some objects made of steel, such as a coat hanger. Obtain a bar magnet and stroke the object in the same direction, making sure to lift the magnet away from the object between strokes. Objects that are attracted to a magnet can be made into temporary magnets. Now design and conduct an experiment to decide which temporary magnet is the strongest.

The magnetic field passes into a steel object, turning it into a magnet. Some stainless steel can be magnetized and some cannot. The temporary magnet's strength can by measured by the number of paper clips it picks up.

Attract or repel?

Background knowledge

On every magnet, the *magnetic poles* are where the force of magnetism is strongest. The north pole of one magnet will always attract the south pole of another magnet. If two south poles or two north poles are placed near one another, they will *repel* each other. When two magnets repel, they push away from one another. Earth is a gigantic magnet – it has a magnetic north and south pole.

Science activity

Look at the pairs of magnets in the pictures. Which pairs will attract each other? Which pairs will repel each other? Circle your answers.

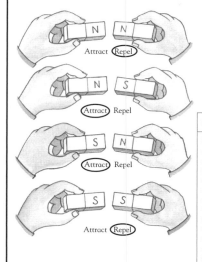

Attract (Repel)

Attract (circled) Repel

(circled) Attract Repel

Attract (Repel)

Science investigation

Obtain 3–4 lifesaver-shaped magnets, and a dowel or pencil that will fit through the magnets' openings. Place the dowel vertically at a base of styrofoam or balsa wood. Try stacking the magnets in different ways on the dowel. Record and explain all of your observations. Do the activity on website **70-1**.

The magnets will either attract or repel when placed on the dowel. When they repel, they look as if they're "floating." As more magnets are added to the dowel, the distance between repelling magnets decreases due to the pull of gravity.

Pushing and pulling

Background knowledge

Forces can make things move. A *force* is a push or pull on something. *Magnetism* is a force that can push (repel) or pull (attract) things. The force of *gravity* pulls objects toward Earth. When the wind blows, you can feel a breeze as air pushes against you. When you drop a ball, the force of gravity pulls it toward Earth.

Science activity

The pictures show a number of forces in action. Decide whether the force is a push or pull. Write your answer beside each picture.

This force is a push.

This force is a push.

This force is a pull.

This force is a pull.

This force is a push.

This force is a pull.

Science investigation

Using a bathroom scale, design and conduct an experiment to see who is the strongest among your family, friends, or classmates. Does a person's size make a difference? Can you push harder with your hand or finger? Does a leg push harder than an arm? Do the activity on website **71-1**.

It is relatively easy for children to understand that pushes and pulls are forces. it's harder to grasp that stretching, bending, turning, and squashing are also examples of forces in action, usually produced by the combined effects of two or more forces.

May the force be with you!

Background knowledge

Forces can make objects at rest begin to move. Forces can also cause moving objects to speed up, slow down, change direction, or stop. Air is a force that pushes against all objects. The pushing force of air is called *air resistance*. A parachute slows down a falling object because of upward-pushing air resistance.

Science activity

Jason and Eduardo were having fun blowing at a ping-pong ball through straws. Draw a line from each picture to the words on the right that explain what will happen to the ping-pong ball.

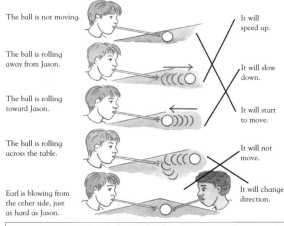

The ball is not moving.

The ball is rolling away from Jason.

The ball is rolling toward Jason.

The ball is rolling across the table.

Earl is blowing from the other side, just as hard as Jason.

It will speed up.

It will slow down.

It will start to move.

It will not move.

It will change direction.

Science investigation

Does a large piece of paper or small piece of paper fall first? Design and conduct an experiment to see what effect air resistance has on different-sized pieces of falling paper. Do the activity on website **72-1**.

Larger pieces of paper will provide more air resistance than smaller pieces of paper, and so will fall more slowly. The young investigator should drop paper of different sizes at the same time. The one that falls at a faster rate has less air resistance.

Friction is forceful

Background knowledge

When you kick a ball, it does not move forever. It gradually slows down and stops. The force that makes the ball slow down is *friction*. Friction is a force that opposes motion. Friction occurs between two surfaces that are touching, such as the surface of the ball and the ground. Some surfaces produce more friction than others.

Science activity

Jamal and Megan rolled marbles down a tube and measured how fast each marble rolled. They tried rolling the marbles over different surfaces. They kept the angle of the tube the same each time. Here are the results.

Surface	Distance marble rolls
Gravel path	21 cm
Grass	3 cm
Kitchen floor	163 cm
Carpet	32 cm
Pavement	85 cm

Which surface produced the most friction?
Grass

How was this surface different from the other surfaces?
It was the roughest surface.

Science investigation

On which surface does a car travel the fastest? Create three ramps out of cardboard or wood. Cover one ramp with fabric or sandpaper. Cover the second with aluminum foil and the third with a material of your choice. Use a book to make an incline. Obtain a small toy car. Design and conduct an experiment to answer the question. Try the activity on website **73-1**.

Small matchbox cars work well for this activity. The rougher the surface, the greater the friction and the slower the car will travel. The child will need a stopwatch. The height of the ramp must be the same for all surfaces tested.

In ship shape

Background knowledge
When a boat moves through water, friction between the bottom of the boat (the hull) and the water slows the boat down. This type of friction is called *drag*. Drag pushes opposite to the boat's movement. The shape of a ship affects how well it can move through the water. Streamlined boats move through water more easily because there is less drag on the boat.

Science activity
Jessica and James made three models of sailboats. Each had a different-shaped hull. In order to create wind for the sails, Jessica used a long cardboard tube to blow them along in a bath of water. James timed how long it took each boat to sail the length of the bathtub.

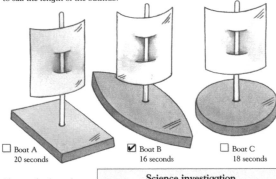

☐ Boat A
20 seconds

☑ Boat B
16 seconds

☐ Boat C
18 seconds

Place a check mark (✔) in the box beside the boat that moved best through the water. Color in the boat with the most streamlined hull.

Science investigation
Try different airplane designs to see which one best reduces drag and creates the most lift. Go to websites **74-1** and **74-2** for design help. Explain how your design reduces drag and creates lift.

The middle boat takes the least time to move through water because its long, pointed hull has the most streamlined shape. Streamlining gives boats, cars, and aircraft smooth shapes so that water or air flows more easily around them, reducing drag.

Pushy things

Background knowledge
It may seem strange, but when you push on an object, it always pushes back at you. When you walk on the floor, the floor pushes back at your feet. When you blow air into a balloon, the walls of the balloon push the air back toward your mouth. It is hard to push a ball under water because as you push down, the water is pushing up against the ball. Everything gets "pushy" when pushed on!

Science activity
The picture at the right shows where the pushing forces are when you push down on a ruler placed at the edge of a table. Draw arrows on the other pictures to show the direction of the pushing forces on each of the objects shown.

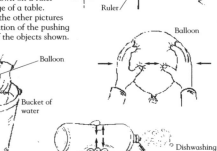

Ruler

Balloon

Balloon

Bucket of water

Dishwashing liquid bottle

Spring

Science investigation
Push down on a table. How does it feel against your hand as you continue to push? Now find a large rubber band (about 30 cm around). Design and conduct an experiment to see whether heavier objects pull with more force than lighter objects.

Forces always work in pairs. When the child pushes down on the desk, the desk will push back with equal force. Therefore, the harder the child pushes, the harder the desk pushes back. This is actually Newton's Law of Action/Reaction.

See the light!

Background knowledge
The light we see with our eyes comes from objects called *light sources*. Light sources include the Sun, flames from candles and fires, and electric lamps. Some animals can produce their own light, such as fireflies and some animals that live near the bottom of the sea. Light always travels in a straight line from a light source to our eyes. (Never look directly at the Sun, because its bright light can cause harm to your eyes.)

Science activity
The picture on the right shows how light from a fluorescent lamp reaches the eyes of the boy. Draw arrows to show how the light reaches the eyes of the children in the pictures below.

Fluorescent lamp

Flashlight

Firefly

Candle

Light bulb

Science investigation
Draw a picture of people in a room with a number of light sources, including one coming from the ceiling. Now draw lines to show the direction in which light travels to the eyes of each person. If all of the lights went out, would the people be able to see anything? Do the activity on website **76-1**.

Light always travels in straight lines. The light coming from the sources in the room spreads out so that many parts of the room are lit up. In order to see objects there must be light reflecting off them, so people cannot see anything in the dark.

The brightest light

Background knowledge
Earth's brightest light source is the *Sun*. The Sun is a star. All stars are composed of gases that are constantly undergoing powerful reactions. When they do, very bright light is produced. There are billions and billions of stars, and even if you counted one star every second for 8 hours a day, after 100 years you would only have counted about a billion! Other stars don't seem as bright as the Sun because they are very far away. Astronomers use numbers called *magnitude numbers* to describe how bright stars look from Earth. Bright stars have low numbers, and faint stars have high numbers. We can see stars with a brightness between magnitudes 1 and 6.

Science activity
Here are some stars with measures of their brightness. Can you place them in order, with the brightest first and the faintest last?

Star	Magnitude
Eri	3.7
Centauri C	11.0
Ross 780	10.2
Procyon A	0.3
Kapteyn's Star	8.8
Sirius B	7.2
Polaris	2.0

Correct order of brightness
1 Procyon A _____ (brightest)
2 Polaris
3 Eri
4 Sirius B
5 Kapteyn's Star
6 Ross 780
7 Centauri C _____ (faintest)

Science investigation
⚠ Suppose you are a scientist studying three stars of different sizes. Make these "stars" by covering a flashlight with a piece of black paper in which you have made three pinpricks of different sizes. Predict which star will be hardest to see as its distance from you increases. Test this out by having a friend shine the flashlight toward you. As your friend walks away from you, is there a distance from which you can no longer see any of the stars? What do you conclude? Explain.

Make sure the paper is opaque so that the only light coming through is from the three different-sized pinpricks. Have the child stand at different distances from the simulated starlight to see how distance affects seeing a star. The child should work with a peer.

See-through materials

Background knowledge
Materials that you can see through, such as glass, are called *transparent* materials. They allow light to pass through them. Materials that you cannot see through, such as steel or concrete, are called *opaque*. Light cannot pass through these materials. Some materials allow some light to pass through them, but the objects on the other side do not appear very clear. These materials are called *translucent*. Wax paper is one translucent material.

Science activity
Fill in the missing words in the table.

Material	Can you see through it?	Can you see the flash-light's light through it?	Scientific description
Aluminum kitchen foil	No	No	Opaque
Kitchen film-wrap	Yes	Yes	Transparent
Greaseproof paper	No	Yes	Translucent
Tissue paper	No	Yes	Translucent
Cardboard	No	No	Opaque
Polythelene bag	No	Yes	Translucent

Science investigation

(!) First, design and conduct an experiment to see what happens to the transparency of water when it freezes. Next, design and conduct an experiment to classify materials found around your home as transparent, translucent, or opaque. Use data tables to summarize your findings.

The child should learn how clearly he or she can see through ice, as compared to liquid water. One possibility is to freeze a small object in water and place the same object in liquid water to see which object is easier to see. Ice becomes translucent.

Tracking shadows

Background knowledge
You cannot see through opaque materials because light will not pass through them. When you place an opaque object between a light source and a wall, a dark area called a *shadow* forms on the wall. The shadow forms because the object stops the light from reaching the wall. Remember, light always travels in a straight line.

Science activity
Vimala taped a cardboard circle to a drinking straw. Next, she held the circle in front of a shining flashlight so that a shadow formed on the wall. Draw the shadow that formed on the wall.

Science investigation

Go to website **79-1** and do the activity about shadows. Now make shadow puppets out of cardboard and glue them to popsicle sticks or straws. Write a play for your puppets and put on a show for your family and friends. Website **79-2** shows how to make shadow puppets.

Shadows are formed by the absence of light. When a flashlight is moved closer to an object, the shadow gets bigger. The angle of the light also affects the length of a shadow. The greater the angle, the longer the shadow will be.

Got light!

Background knowledge
Very few things are sources of light, so why do you see them? Though objects are not sources of light, objects can reflect light. When they do, you can see the objects. You see another person because light is reflected off that person. This light travels into your eyes, where an image of the object is formed. But if there were no light sources, you would not be able to see anything. Devices like lamps were invented to be our light sources at nighttime.

Science activity
Jeremy is sitting at a table reading a book. Draw an arrow to show how Jeremy sees the book on the table.

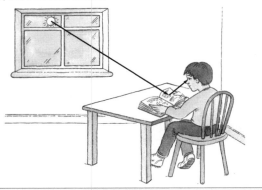

Science investigation

Is it easier to see a silver coin or a copper coin from a long distance? Design and conduct an experiment to see which types of materials are easier to see from a distance. Create a data table to summarize your results.

The experiment should help the child conclude that shinier objects are easier to see. To help explain why, you might ask: Why are objects shiny? *Objects are shiny because they reflect a lot of light. The reflection of light has something to do with seeing objects.*

Sparkle and shine

Background knowledge
Why do some things appear to sparkle while others things do not? Objects that have very smooth surfaces reflect light, which makes them appear shiny. Mirrors reflect light very well. The gems in jewelry sparkle when light is reflected off of them.

Science activity
The picture on the right shows how light reflects off a shiny ring and into the girl's eyes. Use a ruler to draw arrows that show how the light reflects off the shiny things below into the eyes of the children.

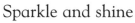
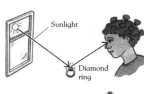
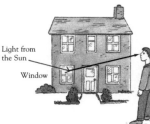
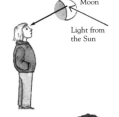

Science investigation

Gather some small objects from around your home. Create your own classification system for these objects based on how shiny they are. For example, you may decide to have three classifications: **not shiny at all**, **somewhat shiny**, and **shiny and sparkling**. What type of materials are the shiniest?

Answers will vary depending on what is collected. Metals will tend to be some of the shiniest objects. Smooth surfaces also tend to be shiny. The shiniest objects appear so because the light they reflect into our eyes is less scattered.

Catch a ray of sunlight

Background knowledge
A mirror has a very shiny surface. Light from a light source reflects off the mirror's surface. The angle at which light hits the mirror is always the same as the angle at which it reflects off of the mirror. Go to website **82-1** to learn more about the behavior of light.

Science activity
Anna used a round mirror to catch the light from the Sun and reflect it onto a fence. On the picture, draw arrows to show how the light reflects off the mirror to form a bright patch on the fence. The arrows should show the incoming light and the reflected light. Use a ruler.

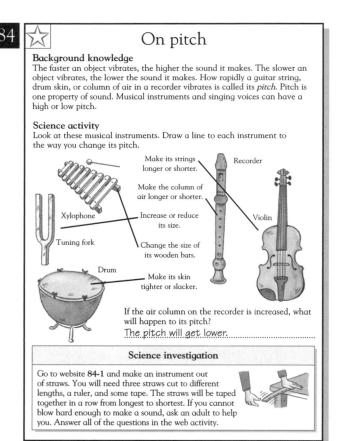

Science investigation

(!) Tape two small mirrors together at an angle and stand them on a table. Now place various objects in front of them. Explain all of your observations. Information about this and other types of kaleidoscopes can be found on websites **82-2** and **82-3**.

The angle at which light strikes a mirror is called the *angle of incidence*. The angle at which light is reflected is called the *angle of reflection*. The angle of incidence always equals the angle of reflection.

Sounds of music

Background knowledge
Sound is made when objects vibrate. We say that an object vibrates when it moves back and forth quickly. All musical instruments have parts that vibrate to make sound. Instruments such as the guitar have strings that vibrate when played, while wind instruments such as the flute have a column of air that vibrates when you blow into them. Some instruments have special parts that vibrate when struck with an object or hand.

Science activity
Place an X on the part of the instrument that vibrates to create a musical sound.

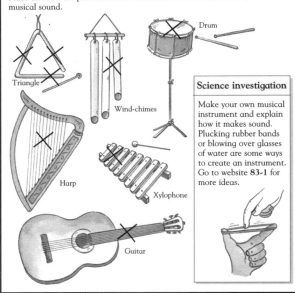

Science investigation

Make your own musical instrument and explain how it makes sound. Plucking rubber bands or blowing over glasses of water are some ways to create an instrument. Go to website **83-1** for more ideas.

The child learns that sounds are made when objects vibrate. It is easy to "see sound" when plucked guitar strings vibrate or rubber band "instruments" are plucked. After the child makes a musical instrument, ask him or her what is creating the sound.

On pitch

Background knowledge
The faster an object vibrates, the higher the sound it makes. The slower an object vibrates, the lower the sound it makes. How rapidly a guitar string, drum skin, or column of air in a recorder vibrates is called its *pitch*. Pitch is one property of sound. Musical instruments and singing voices can have a high or low pitch.

Science activity
Look at these musical instruments. Draw a line to each instrument to the way you change its pitch.

Make its strings longer or shorter.

Make the column of air longer or shorter.

Increase or reduce its size.

Change the size of its wooden bars.

Make its skin tighter or slacker.

Xylophone
Tuning fork
Drum
Recorder
Violin

If the air column on the recorder is increased, what will happen to its pitch?
The pitch will get lower.

Science investigation

Go to website **84-1** and make an instrument out of straws. You will need three straws cut to different lengths, a ruler, and some tape. The straws will be taped together in a row from longest to shortest. If you cannot blow hard enough to make a sound, ask an adult to help you. Answer all of the questions in the web activity.

After doing this activity, the child will see how the pitch of sound can be modified by changing the length of the vibrating area. The longer the length, the lower the pitch. The child can have fun trying to play a tune on the straws.

Good vibrations

Background knowledge
When you blow over the neck of a bottle, the air inside vibrates and makes a sound. The more air there is in the bottle, the slower it vibrates and the lower the pitch of the sound. Adding water to the bottle reduces the amount of air and raises the pitch. The pitch is also higher if you use a smaller bottle, which holds less air. All wind instruments work by making the air inside of them vibrate.

Science activity
Sean made a wind instrument from a drinking straw. He flattened one end of the straw and cut both sides so that it formed a V-shape. When he blew into the cut end of the straw, it vibrated. The vibrations caused the air inside the straw to vibrate and make a sound. See website **85-1**.

What do you think happened to the pitch of the sound when Sean cut the straw in half?
The pitch became higher.

Science investigation

(!) Design and conduct an experiment to see if you can play a tune on bottles filled with water. Add a different amount of water to a number of identical bottles. Each bottle should make a sound of a different pitch when you blow over the neck. Adjust the water levels in the bottles until you get sounds you like. If you have any respiratory problem, ask for help from an adult.

The pitch of any reed or wind instrument can be changed by altering the length of air inside it. The shorter the air column, the faster it vibrates when you blow into the instrument, and the higher the pitch of the notes produced.

Loud or soft?

Background knowledge
In addition to pitch, *loudness* is another property of sound. If you hit a cymbal softly, it makes a soft sound. If you hit it hard, it makes a loud sound. The harder you pluck a guitar string, the louder the sound it makes. The harder you blow a whistle, the louder the sound it makes. All musical instruments work in the same way.

Science activity
Michael put some grains of rice on the skin of a tambourine. When he beat the tambourine, the rice jumped up and down as the skin vibrated. Learn more at website **86-1**.

What do you think will happen to the rice grains if Michael beats the tambourine harder?

They jumped higher.

Science investigation
Make a simple instrument called a kazoo by folding tissue paper over the teeth of a comb. To play the kazoo, you press it to your mouth and hum through it with your lips close together. Design and conduct an experiment to see how you can make the kazoo produce sounds of varying loudness.

The child will learn to change the volume of a sound. Beating a tambourine harder makes the vibrations larger and so increases the volume of the sound. However, it does not change the number or speed of the vibrations, so the pitch stays the same.

Feel the vibrations!

Background knowledge
When a person sings, the vocal cords in the throat make the air vibrate (move back and forth). These vibrations travel through the air to your ears. You hear the vibrating air as sounds. Try feeling the vibrations in your throat when you sing. *Sound* is a type of energy that always travels as vibrations.

Science activity
Here are two children using a string walkie-talkie. The sentences below explain how the boy can hear the girl speak, but they are not in the correct order. Write the numbers 1–5 in the boxes to show what the correct order should be.

3 The string vibrates.

5 The vibrations are heard by the ear.

1 The girl's vocal cords vibrate.

2 The air vibrates in the girl's container.

4 The air vibrates in the boy's container.

Science investigation
⚠ Make your own walkie-talkie with two plastic cups or soup cans and some string or wire. Ask an adult to punch a hole in the cup or can. Pull the wire or string through the holes and then wrap the ends around small paper clips so they cannot slip back. Design and conduct an experiment to see if a person can hear you through the cup or can. Explain how the sound travels.

As the child talks into the can, the air vibrates, causing the can to vibrate. This then vibrates the string, transmitting sound across the string to the other can. As the second can vibrates, the air in the can vibrates and the other child hears the sound.

Quiet please!

Background knowledge
Sound travels through any material that will vibrate. Some materials, such as metals, vibrate easily and carry sound well. These materials are called *sound conductors*. Other materials, such as rubber, do not vibrate very much and thus do not carry sound as well. These materials are called *sound insulators*.

Science activity
Maria and Brian tested materials to see which was the best sound insulator. One by one, Maria covered her ears with a material and closed her eyes. Brian read out 20 numbers, and Maria called out the numbers she heard. Each time, Brian stood the same distance away and spoke with the same loud voice.

Material	How many numbers Maria heard
Rubber	16
Thick cotton wool	11
Thick wool	12
Thick plastic	17
Polystyrene	12
Hands	10

Science investigation
Design and conduct an experiment to see what material best blocks the sound of a ticking clock. Place a battery-operated clock with a loud ticking noise in a box. Experiment by placing different materials over the box to see which one can best block the ticking sounds. You could also use a small portable radio or any other device that makes a steady noise. Do the activity on website **88-1**.

Which material was the best insulator?

Maria's hands

Dense materials, such as hands, are good sound insulators because they do not vibrate very much. Any material that does not vibrate well, such as foam, can be an insulator. Encourage the child to test a number of materials.

A whale of a story

Background knowledge
In air, sound travels more than 300 meters every second (about 750 miles per hour). In water, it travels five times faster, at about 1,500 meters every second. Whales use their vocal cords to make sounds. They also have a very good sense of hearing. The sounds that they make travel for thousands of kilometers through the oceans and can be heard by other whales far away.

Science activity
The figures in the table on the right show how many meters sound travels every second in different materials. Use the information in the table to decide which of the statements below are true and which are false. Place a check mark (✔) beside the statements that you think are true.

Material	Speed of sound (meters per second)
Cold air	330
Warm air	350
Fresh water	1,410
Ocean water	1,540
Steel	5,060
Granite rock	6,000

☑ Whales in the ocean hear sounds more quickly than goldfish in a lake.

☐ It is easier to hear sounds in winter than in summer.

☐ Railway workers hear the horn of an approaching express train before they hear the vibrations it makes in the steel rails.

☐ You hear sounds more quickly in gases than in liquids.

☑ It is possible to hear sounds through rocks.

Science investigation
⚠ Using two balloons, one filled with water and the other with air, design and conduct an experiment to see if you can hear better through air or water. Make sure the balloons are the same size.

The speed of sound is affected by the medium through which it travels. Sound travels faster through denser materials. Temperature also affects the speed of sound. The child should observe that it is easier to hear through water than air.

Getting in shape with Earth

Background knowledge
Stars and planets have a round shape called a *sphere*. *Stars* are balls of gases that produce heat and light. Our solar system contains a star called the Sun. Planets are made of rock, gas, and sometimes frozen liquid. Some planets have natural satellites called *moons* that travel around them. Our solar system has nine planets. A satellite is an object that travels around a larger object. Some scientists think there may be a tenth planet.

Science activity
Imagine you are traveling in a spacecraft and are able to look out of the window at out part of the solar system. Which of these pictures would you be most likely to see? Place a check mark (✔)in the right box.

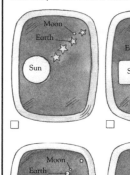
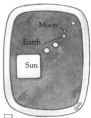
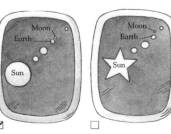

Science investigation

To take a tour of our solar system go to website **90-1**. These other websites are fun to visit: **90-2, 90-3, 90-4** (the last one has a scale model of our solar system and includes information on the possible tenth planet).

These are outstanding introductory websites about our solar system. The child will learn that the Sun, Earth and Moon are all spherical. While children this age do not need to know the names of all of the planets, they may find them interesting.

Sunrise, sunset

Background knowledge
You have likely noticed that the Sun changes its position in the sky throughout the day. During sunrise it is in one place and at sunset it is located on the opposite side of the sky. The Sun appears to move across the sky during the day, but it is not the Sun that is moving. Our planet does the moving! As Earth turns around, we see the Sun as we pass by it. This motion is why the Sun appears to rise in the east and set in the west. Go to website **91-1** to learn more.

Science activity
Samantha drew a picture of the Sun on a piece of paper. In the morning, she attached the picture to the window over where she could see the Sun shining. (She was careful not to look directly at the Sun.) Draw where you think she had to put the picture in the afternoon.

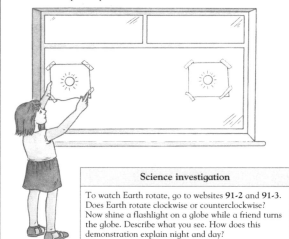

Science investigation

To watch Earth rotate, go to websites **91-2** and **91-3**. Does Earth rotate clockwise or counterclockwise? Now shine a flashlight on a globe while a friend turns the globe. Describe what you see. How does this demonstration explain night and day?

The child should understand is that night and day are caused by Earth's motion. As it rotates counterclockwise, the Sun appears to rise in the east and set in the west. The globe investigation illustrates this well, for not all of "Earth" is can be illuminated at once.

Me and my shadow

Background knowledge
The Sun is a very powerful light source. When sunlight shines on a wall, it makes the wall bright. If you place a solid, opaque object in front of the wall, the sunlight cannot pass through it and a shadow forms on the wall. Because Earth is rotating, the Sun seems to move across the sky, casting different shadows from morning (sunrise) to evening (sunset).

Science activity
The morning Sun was shining through the window in Tony's home, casting an interesting shadow of a vase on the table. Tony thought it looked great, and wanted to show his father when he came home from work. If there was still sunlight coming through the window in the afternoon, draw how the shadow looked when Tony showed it to his father.

Science investigation

On a sunny day, find your shadow on the ground. Try to change its shape. At what time in the day is your shadow the longest? Go to websites **92-1** and **92-2** to learn more.

The child will learn that his or her outdoor shadow moves as the day progresses. As the Sun appears to move across the sky, the position and length of the shadow will change. Shadows in the morning and evening are longer than those cast at midday.

Is the Moon out tonight?

Background knowledge
It takes the Moon about 28 days to travel around Earth. It travels around Earth in a counterclockwise direction. It rises and sets during the night, just as the Sun rises and sets during the day. On Earth, the Moon appears to rise in the east and set in the west. Because of the way the Moon moves, we are only able to see one side of it.

Science activity
In this picture, it is evening and a boy and girl are looking at the Moon. Draw where you think they may see the Moon later that night.

Science investigation

⚠ Go to website **93-1** to see Moon photography. What are some of the features of the Moon? Does the Moon change shape in the evening sky? Explain. Is there a man on the Moon? Go to website **93-2** to find out. Go to website **93-3** to explore the Moon with the Apollo astronauts.

The child learns that the Moon makes one complete rotation on its axis during each orbit around Earth. The Moon does not produce its own light. It reflects light from the Sun. The Moon changes shape in the evening sky during a month.

Day and night

Background knowledge
As Earth spins, it makes one complete turn every 24 hours. Whenever our part of Earth turns to face the Sun, the Sun lights it up, giving us daytime. Whenever Earth turns away from the Sun, sunlight can no longer reach us. It gets dark, giving us nighttime. Day turns to night and night turns to day as Earth constantly spins around.

Science activity
Here is a picture of Earth as it appears from space. Draw an arrow on the picture to show from which direction the Sun is shining on Earth.

Science investigation

Go to website **94-1** and turn Earth to create daytime and nighttime. Go to website **94-2** to see pictures of Earth at nighttime. In your own words, explain why there is daytime and nighttime.

The child learns that day and night are caused by the motion of Earth as it spins on its axis every 24 hours. The web pictures of Earth at night show how lit up (industrialized) some parts of the world are.

The light of the Moon

Background knowledge
As the Moon travels around Earth, we see different amounts of the Moon lit up by the Sun. This is known as the *phases of the Moon*. When the Moon is lit up and is round, it is called a *full moon*. The amount of the Moon's sunlit side we see, gradually shrinks or wanes. When the Moon is not lit up by the Sun, it is called a *new moon*. During a new moon, you cannot see the Moon in the sky. After a new moon, the amount we can see of the sunlit side grows, or waxes, each night until it is a full moon again.

Science activity
Draw a line from each of the phases below to show its correct position in the sequence from new moon to new moon. (A gibbous phase is when about three-quarters of the Moon is lit up.)

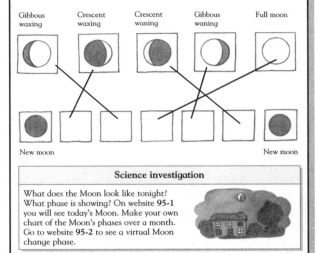

Science investigation

What does the Moon look like tonight? What phase is showing? On website **95-1** you will see today's Moon. Make your own chart of the Moon's phases over a month. Go to website **95-2** to see a virtual Moon change phase.

The child learns that the Moon changes as it orbits Earth. The first website shows what the Moon looks like in real time and the second shows a simulation of the motion of the Moon. Adjust it to show the view from Earth.

Referenced websites

Cigarette health problems	16-2	http://thescooponsmoking.org/xhtml/effectsHome.php
Plant growth	17-1	www.bbc.co.uk/schools/scienceclips/ages/7_8/plants_grow.shtml
Bean experiment	18-1	http://wow.osu.edu/experiments/plants/roots.html
Seed experiment	18-2	www.kidzone.ws/science/seeds.htm
Identifying leaves	19-1	www.cnr.vt.edu/dendro/forsite/idleaf.htm
More on identifying leaves	19-2	www.oplin.org/tree/leaf/byleaf.html
Non-flowering plants	20-1	www.urbanext.uiuc.edu/gpe/case3/facts.html
More non-flowering plants	20-2	www.zephyrus.co.uk/nonfloweringplants.html
Flowering plants	20-3	www.backyardnature.net/fpdefine.htm
Venn diagram for flowering and non-flowering plants	20-4	www.abcteach.com/Plants/venn.htm
Seeds	21-1	www.urbanext.uiuc.edu/gpe/case3/c3facts1.html
Pumpkin science	22-1	www.monroe2boces.org/programs.cfm?subpage=458&searchfor=pumpkins
Factors for plant growth	23-1	www.bbc.co.uk/schools/scienceclips/ages/7_8/plants_grow.shtml
Animal groups	24-1	www.lethsd.ab.ca/mmh/grade3c/Gr3Web/Animals/animal_groups.htm
Electronic zoo	24-2	http://netvet.wustl.edu/pix.htm
Plant groups	25-1	http://yorkcountyschools.org/mes/plant%20webquest/Plant%20Characteristics.htm
Flower types	25-2	http://community.webshots.com/slideshow?ID=320840762&key=bxklQh
Interdependence of life key	26-1	www.bbc.co.uk/schools/scienceclips/ages/10_11/interdependence.shtml
State butterflies	26-2	www.npwrc.usgs.gov/resource/distr/lepid/bflyusa/bflyusa.htm
Squash	27-1	http://whatscookingamerica.net/squash.htm
Practice in using a branching key	27-2	http://webworld.freac.fsu.edu/cameras/keys/sa/tree.html
Pollution	28-1	http://tiki.oneworld.net/penguin/pollution/pollution2.html
Human activity and pollution	28-2	www.niehs.nih.gov/kids/baylor/earth1.htm
Habitats	29-1	http://library.thinkquest.org/11234/
More on habitats	29-2	http://mbgnet.mobot.org/
Habitat activity	29-3	www.bbc.co.uk/schools/scienceclips/ages/8_9/habitats.shtml
Habitat activity 2	29-4	www.on.ec.gc.ca/greatlakeskids/habitatfinal.html
Hatch brine shrimp	30-1	www.lawrencehallofscience.org/foss/fossweb/teachers/materials/plantanimal/brineshrimp.html
Adaptations	30-2	www.uen.org/utahlink/activities/view_activity.cgi?activity_id=4750
Comparing skulls and teeth	31-1	www.d91.k12.id.us/www/skyline/teachers/robertsd/mammal1.htm
Dinosaur puppets	31-2	www.rain.org/~philfear/download-a-dinosaur.html
Food chain activity	32-1	www.bbc.co.uk/schools/scienceclips/ages/8_9/habitats.shtml
Information about food chains	32-2	www.gould.edu.au/foodwebs/kids_web.htm

CONCEPT MAP GRAPHIC ORGANIZER

What does the word mean?

Give examples:

1.

2.

3.

Write the word:

Complete this organizer for each italicized word on the worksheets. This will help you better understand the science word or concept.

What is the word related to?

1.

2.

3.

Use the word in sentences:

CONCEPT MAP GRAPHIC ORGANIZER

Example

What does the word mean?

The force that pulls things toward Earth.

Give examples:

1. A ball falls down.

2. When I jump, I fall down.

3. A rock falls to the bottom of a river.

Write the word:

Gravity

What is the word related to?

1. Forces

2. Weight

3. Mass

Use the word in sentences:

1. My weight is caused by the pull of **gravity**.

2. The pull of **gravity** is less on the Moon because it has less mass than Earth.

3. Objects fall to Earth because of the pull of **gravity**.

Inquiry template
INSTRUCTIONS

Name ....

QUESTION
State your testable question.
Testable question: Who? Why? Where? When? How?
This is a question that can be answered by conducting an experiment.

PREDICTION (hypothesis)
This is a statement about what you think may happen in the experiment. It is not a guess, but is based on things you have observed or previous experiments you have conducted. Give an explanation for your prediction.

EXPERIMENTAL PROCEDURE
A well-designed experimental procedure includes:
- *Directions:* Steps to follow to conduct the experiment.
- *Materials:* A list of all materials that will be used in the experiment.
- *Variable(s):* Identified variables. (1) Which variable will you manipulate (change)? (2) What is your responding variable? (3) Which variables will remain constant in your experiment?
- *Data collection:* Tables, graphs, charts, etc. for data organization. Include measurements in your data when you can.
- *Large sample size or repeated trials:* Good experiments have large sample sizes and/or are repeated a number of times.

RESULT
This is a statement made after analyzing the data collected. It identifies any patterns seen in the data. Do the patterns support the prediction (hypothesis)?

CONCLUSION
This is a summary that states whether the prediction (hypothesis) was proven. It explains why the prediction was proven or disproven.

COMMUNICATE RESULT
- Share your findings with others and ask for their analysis of your findings.
- Write a report or design a storyboard to tell about your investigation.

Elementary level

Inquiry template
INSTRUCTIONS

Name _____ Date _____

QUESTION
State your testable question.

PREDICTION (hypothesis)

EXPERIMENTAL PROCEDURE

Approved by: _____

Elementary level

Certificate

Elementary Grades 3–4 Level

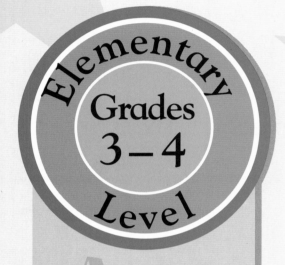

Science

Congratulations to

...................................(Name)

for successfully finishing this book.

Well done!

Age.................Date.................